Live and Love

Live and Love

✦

Family Lessons

Edna Kaye

iUniverse, Inc.
New York Lincoln Shanghai

Live and Love
Family Lessons

iUniverse books may be ordered through booksellers or by contacting:

iUniverse
2021 Pine Lake Road, Suite 100
Lincoln, NE 68512
www.iuniverse.com
1-800-Authors (1-800-288-4677)

ISBN-13: 978-0-595-37073-3 (pbk)
ISBN-13: 978-0-595-81473-2 (ebk)
ISBN-10: 0-595-37073-X (pbk)
ISBN-10: 0-595-81473-5 (ebk)

Printed in the United States of America

Contents

1

GRANDMOTHERS

Grandmother's old farm was twelve miles from the city. The grounds were beautiful, with apple and cherry orchards, tennis courts, and a huge old barn with a hayloft. In retrospect, I realize it was luxury farming. A jersey cow provided the milk. Chickens were raised to furnish eggs and Sunday dinner. I used to hide on Saturdays when it came time for George to catch the young broilers and wring their necks. A sudden stillness followed the frenzied cackling. Sister and I were allowed to gather eggs. Since hens and roosters are unpredictable in their line of flight, it was frightening.

The house itself was not large, but the rooms were interesting. Good friends and family gathered for fun, talk, and meals in the combination living-dining area, furnished in massive golden oak. Formal business callers or tiresome ladies were ushered into the dark, musty front parlor. This guaranteed the brevity of the visit.

German Rosie cooked in the large kitchen, the real hub of the farm. Rosie had come from the old country at age fourteen and was devoted to Grandmother. Often the two women battled, shouting in German. However, their mutual admiration held fast. Rosie baked bread and coffee cake each weekend. On special occasions, she prepared home-made noodles, rolling the dough paper thin. Then, with her long, sharp knife, sliced the sheet into narrow strips.

Milk from "old Bossy" was brought to the kitchen and poured into the blue milk pails to set for a while before skimming. If I timed it right and caught up with George at milking time, he would "pull" a cup of fresh, warm milk for me, cream and all.

Guest rooms upstairs were called the blue room and the rose room because of the colorings in the wallpaper and decorations. On each chiffonier stood a large basin with matching pitcher. Under each bed was a potty. I don't know where Rosie or George slept at night. I do know there was an outhouse for their toilet and a large rain barrel from which Rosie scooped water to wash. I imagine George didn't bathe too often.

The "Old Farm" was used only in the summer, but it was a hive of bustling activity every day of those warm months. Vegetables from the garden were canned for winter. Red juicy strawberries were mixed with sugar and put in the sun to set—sunshine strawberry jam. Many scarecrows were scattered throughout the orchard. Bells dangled from branches to keep the birds from stripping the cherry trees. Every sour cherry was picked for canning. There was always a ladder handy to get your fill of the sweet ones.

At Grandmother's "Old Farm," I first learned to ride my two-wheel bicycle. This was not a simple feat because the driveway was gravel and skiddy. Only on gasless Sundays were we allowed to ride on the road.

On Saturdays, added to the excitement of the chicken-killing ritual, was another important event, Mr. Button Peddler arrived. He had a large satchel with trays containing buttons of all sizes, pins, needles, and thread. Grandmother always bought the dry goods from him. I don't know how far he had to come to get there, but he walked.

Dr. Cooke, the minister, lived across the street. Next door to him was a poor family with several children. Because Agnes, the eldest girl, monopolized sister Barby, I hated her, felt she was a bad influence. They spent most of their time eluding me. I was hurt, but stubborn enough to persist in following them. Once Agnes tore her skirt on a fence and borrowing needle and thread, she promptly mended it with tiny almost invisible stitches. Mother was startled, and we were shocked. Whenever I think of Agnes, I think of the old proverb, "A stitch in time—"

Grandmother was a handsome woman of regal appearance with thick, snowy hair piled high on her head. Aquiline nose, smallish pale eyes, and a fine-grained skin completed the picture. Only the brown spots on the back of her tapered hands marred their beauty. Daily she scrubbed her fingernails, later buffing them with a pink powder to make them shiny. Unkempt hands were not tolerated. An old-fashioned corset girdled her portly body, giving her no figure at all. Grandmother didn't worry about weight and ate heartily.

Many of her acquaintances were scared by her stern manner. The one time she seemed to unbend was when we were sick. If we were getting a cold, she personally put us to bed and served us hot lemonade. Somehow it always helped.

After Grandfather died, she was intolerant of dogs and cats, but had a canary, a "Dickie." Here she really let go. Dickie was allowed unlimited freedom, perching on the rim of a goblet, pecking from the sugar bowl. With crazy abandonment he flew from the first floor to the second. The cage door was open during the day so the bird could come and go at will. At night, a black, weighted cloth was tossed over the cage to assure a good night's sleep for both canary and house occupant.

Aunt Kate, Grandmother's sister, came to live at 2877 Fleming Boulevard. Also she was a regular visitor of "the old farm" in earlier days. No one explained Aunt Kate, a tiny woman with one leg and crutches. There were hints from Mother that the loss of the leg had shattered marriage chances for the once vivacious Kate. This quality was hard to imagine because my great aunt was now colorless both in personality and looks. White hair was pushed under a tight hairnet unbecomingly. Pale lips matched the paper-like surface of her face.

Her hands appeared large, the fingers twisted and gnarled. Nevertheless, she was able to crochet and did so constantly. I have a treasured bedspread she made of hundreds of crocheted medallions put together. I don't think the sisters enjoyed each other's company, but both would have been lonely apart.

Dad's mother was a widow for many years. Of necessity she learned to do her own checkbook, gaining intelligence in business matters. This impressed me. My mother dismissed all mundane things like banking, neglecting to enter amount or payee. Not so Grandmother, who with sufficient funds to live comfortably, still was thrifty, budgeting her income carefully.

Just recently, I was obliged to go through cartons of papers stored in the company warehouse. I found it time consuming but revealing, scanning the checkbooks dating back to 1916. Grandfather's financial records clearly depicted his ease and confidence with money. Half the time he scorned most of the arithmetic, entering only the amount of the check. In contrast, Grandmother carefully subtracted and balanced her book to the penny.

Money had to exchange hands. This much Grandmother would concede. But it had to be clean. She demanded and received new money, whether from the bank or in change from a purchase. "I gave you crisp, new bills," she would say.

"I want new ones back."

Christmas always posed a problem. No one knew what to buy for Grandmother. Pretense was not one of her characteristics. If the gift was all wrong, you knew it in a hurry. Aunt Susie usually failed. The time Susie presented her with a woolen shawl was the worst. Its tone was muddy green too, so she couldn't even admire the color.

Grandmother worried about no heirs to carry on the family name. Apparently producing sister and myself was not adequate. Once she confided she wished Mother had tried harder. Therefore, when my first child was a boy, she was delighted. She scared him by clucking too loudly and by clapping her hands vigorously. I never could make her understand that tiny babies can be frightened by sudden noises. "I think it's the black gloves that he doesn't like," she would say.

When I was a child, Grandmother awed me with her brusque manners and blunt speech. I was afraid to play in her house, it was so neat. However, she did have interesting books, a collection of old Harpers bound together. These were full of fairy stories, history, articles, and a wealth of entertainment.

Grandmother had an electric car that she wheeled about the city streets. A bud vase in a corner always held a fresh posy. In later years, she had a chauffeur who kept her black limousine dust free. There was a gasoline pump in the garage so there was no excuse for being low on fuel. Often she took Kate or a friend and rode to the country to Mr. Kaniddle's farm for fresh corn, to the cemetery, or just to the movies. Riding in her car, a velvety robe over her knees, was one of her valued pleasures.

When I was about fifteen, I overheard Mother declining an invitation for me to accompany Grandmother to Atlantic City. No one was more delighted than Father when he heard me express a desire to go. In fact, he had become sensitive about our obvious preference to Mother's side of the family. Enjoying the selfishness of youth, I was not the least concerned with Grandmother, but anticipated a break from parents, a chance to meet some vacationing young people. I suspected, and rightly, that she would be at a loss to set any dating rules. So off we went, both secretly pleased with the arrangement.

In those days, Atlantic City was the spot to go during spring vacation, much as Fort Lauderdale, Daytona or Nassau are today. Grandmother stayed at the Marlboro Blenheim Hotel where she was known and was treated like royalty. Frugal by nature, she was not lavish in tips or spectacular in her dress, but always commanded respect. We took long rides on the boardwalk in carriages pushed by a cyclist, a unique attraction of Atlantic City.

Our Grandmother remained in mourning for her husband for thirty years, never deviating from white or black dresses or accessories. The most important part of the day focused around the choosing of an outfit to complement her beautiful hair.

At night we dined together, first parading up and down "Peacock's Alley," a long, prominent corridor of the hotel. Here she nudged me saying, "See, they're admiring my white hair and your blondness. We make quite a pair."

Embarrassed, I blushed anxiously, but was helpless to do anything. If it boosted her ego to think she was the star attraction, I decided I could weather the ordeal. After sitting in the lobby a while, she retired early. Then I was free to join the younger group.

There was nothing subtle about this arrangement, no distinction between tact and frankness. There was no sense in getting your feelings hurt. That was Grandmother. If, by a supreme effort, she tried to gloss over, it showed in her face anyway. This bluntness automatically eliminated all the misunderstandings that come from nuances and concealments. In later years, my husband once told me, "You spend so much time trying to please everyone, you end up pleasing no one." Maybe it's better to be cruelly outspoken—I don't know.

Grandmother was a string saver and one who methodically folded crumpled tissue paper and saved it. I have always been a box saver. Perhaps this came from observing Grandmother's hall drawers. There were four banks of them, neat and organized with string tightly wound in a ball or on cardboard. In the next drawer lay the stacks of neatly folded used tissue, then the assorted boxes and rubber bands. Ribbon also was kept, pressed, and pinned on a spool, ready to use.

This same preciseness carried over to the linens. From their trip around the world, Grandfather had lavishly bought many tablecloths, some heavily embroidered. Others were delicately worked Chinese ones. These cloths were rolled on bamboo poles to prevent wrinkling, and then stored in the magic hall closet. I suppose Rosie did the ironing of these priceless treasures. Living-room drapes were cleaned by tossing them in a bag of cornmeal mixture, which was supposed to absorb the dirt. They looked clean so I guess it worked. Net and lace curtains were washed by hand and put on pin stretchers to eliminate ironing.

Punctuality was a fetish with Grandmother. "Trains won't wait for you, Edna," she cautioned, as we sat in the station a full hour ahead of schedule. Breakfast was at eight, luncheon at one, and dinner at seven. Train, hotel or home—nothing could change that. If I didn't jump to my feet in the morning, she shook me smartly until she was sure I was awake.

One time, in Florida, I stayed on the beach longer than usual and arrived in the dining room at one twenty. From the ensuing scene, I learned to wear a watch or else not go. For appointments, she managed to arrive fifteen minutes early. During many years, this strictness of schedule made me so time conscious, I became impatient with tardy people.

My memories of Grandfather are hazy because he died at an early age. Short of stature, gray-haired, he wore rimless glasses, which could not hide the twinkle in his eye. He loved people, was outgoing, and friendly.

At the "old farm", they never knew whether there would be six or twenty-six for Sunday night supper. Much depended on where Grandfather had been that week. Cordials were served in tiny crystal glasses. Everyone felt welcome and comfortable. I don't recall that Grandfather ever came to our house, but we went there. I remember bouncing on his knee, eating horehound candy from a glass jar by his leather chair.

Father adored his dad, and his admiration increased with the passing of years. Going through old letters recently I came upon many which showed me how clever and diplomatic the gentleman was. These grandparents traveled extensively, wintered in Florida, and left the business details to my father at home. Grandfather wrote glowing letters of praise, heaping compliments that made Father work harder to live up to the picture.

Stern and unemotional, it was hard to picture Grandmother giving in to the weakness of tears. However, the visits to the cemetery revealed a hidden aspect of her nature.

"Come, Edna," she called, "It's Saturday and we want to go to the cemetery."

A man drove us, using Grandmother's special key to unlock the gates. Grandmother stood motionless at the grave, saying a small prayer. These visits to the graveside seemed to give her some spiritual nourishment even though she had never been a churchwoman.

"I don't want you ever to forget your Grandfather, Edna," she would say. "He had more friends than anyone in town and was good to everyone. He gave not only money to every cause, but gave of himself," she continued. "We had glorious years together. Your Grandfather always laughed at my thriftiness. When we traveled around the world, he insisted on buying the finest silks and laces for me, generous to a fault."

Many times I went to stay with our other grandmother whom we called Nannie. Papa, my mother's father, was sweet but frail, indecisive with large, watery eyes. One sensed that the unkempt handlebar mustache he sported gave him a feeling of security. Theirs was a modest home in the suburbs, and they lived on a limited income.

Papa was a dentist and dentist fees were low in those days. Miss Viet was his loyal assistant who did the cleaning and changed cotton. A clean, scrubbed woman, she had huge facial pores, which must have required extra scouring to even make her presentable. I think she used henna on her hair, a fact I'm sure Papa never suspected. Despite his passivism, he had definite ideas on purity of women. "A woman who will smoke will do anything," he reported ominously to me once. I was naive, uninformed, and the "anything" conjured up pictures of stripping to robbing a bank.

Papa's only luxury was a car. Most evenings he sat in his chair reading, studying checkers or playing solitaire. He chewed tobacco and kept a brass spittoon by his chair.

Only on Sundays was the car wheeled out. Papa was a horrible driver. It was a terrifying experience to go for a ride. Precarious enough to get the sedan backed out of the one-car garage, but once out on the street, it was a true menace. Nannie knew nothing about automobiles nor did she want to.

But she so loved Papa that if he thought he could take us for a Sunday drive, who was she to doubt it? We stalled, we jerked, we either went too fast or too slow. Papa never quite got the hang of it. I guess it is why he walked to the street-car each day of the workweek.

There was no particular goal on these rides. People just went for drives in the country on Sunday afternoons, sometimes just to look. I believe Papa was not too confident of his driving ability either. For example, in snowy weather, any thought of a trip was abandoned.

If Nannie spied a place she wanted to stop, it was a major project, often requiring the services of all of us. I think everyone concerned was relieved when the car was back at home base. Automatically, the passengers jumped out to help wash off the country dirt. Then it was another tense period to get the black monster safely in the garage. There was a big cement bump to negotiate at the entrance. This was a scary moment, getting Papa over that, yet stopping before he went through the other end. Nervously, he raced the motor before making the attempt, so there was no danger of stalling. If this happened, it presented another momentous decision, whether to back up or warily continue forward. When it finally came to a sputtering rest, the auto was covered with an old cozy blanket to keep it clean for the next week.

Papa was never very strong. Bouts of pleurisy kept him thin. This was partly the reason everyone humored him. Papa's jokes were repetitious and corny. Pretending he was putting a green filling in a tooth by mistake was one of his favorite jests. Listeners flattered him by laughing, so I did the same.

Life was fun at Nannie's. Many of the things I know today, I learned from her. Nannie was an excellent listener, a marvelous storyteller. Tales were biblical or of her own childhood days. Motherless from birth, Nannie was raised by four aunts with no squandered love and few toys. I was fascinated and secretly ashamed of our own playroom full of dolls and games.

Born in a small country town in Ohio, she grew up in a frame house near a brook. Here was her play yard, the moss on the old tree trunk, the jewel green carpet, the toadstools, twigs, her doll furniture and "people." When it was our turn to talk, Nannie would let us recite poems while she played sad, accompanying music at the piano. We would weep with the sheer beauty of it all.

Nannie stood tall and straight. Formerly a fiery redhead, she had inherited a matching temper, which she had learned to control. One time, when I became impatient with a stubborn look, she made me sit down on a stool at the foot of her rocker.

"Edna," she said. "There are many things we must learn in this life. We all have bad habits and shortcomings to overcome."

"How can I help it when I get mad?" I asked.

"I had a very bad temper when I was young," she answered.

"Always stop and think before you speak in anger. Two people can't argue if one stays silent. It's very difficult to carry on a fight if no one fights back." This advice has helped me countless times. I have tried to give the message to my children.

Life with Papa remained meager, but the little house on Cory road was filled with love and understanding. Every morning Nannie accompanied him to the corner where he caught the streetcar. Every evening, she was waiting at the window or at the door for his return.

In later years her health was poor, but she did not allow herself to stoop. Her hair was pulled back in a knot, and the white in it was yellowed. Dentures didn't fit properly and clicked noisily when she ate. Ears were too long, eyebrows too bushy. But, so full of love and compassion was her face, that the physical defects were forgotten.

Nannie taught me to make a good apple pie. There were no rules and no measuring. The tricks of success were there if you just watched the process. Bread and butter, sprinkled with sugar—cambric tea, were the standard after-school snacks when I stayed there. Disinterested in housework of any kind, she often left the dishes in the sink while she looked through a box of old letters.

While a houseguest there, much of my time was spent trying to clean or produce some semblance of order. Nannie was not offended or even much interested. When I found moths in the old stuffed owl mounted on the wall, she just laughed. An open sleeping porch was their bedroom. Instead of using a bedspread, they used a down comforter that made the lumpy double bed look uneven but cozy. I often took naps there or in the pansy room. In this small guest room was a picture of multicolored pansies. After long scrutiny, they became persons to me, each with a distinct identity. Once I had acknowledged them as such, I could no longer recognize them as flowers.

My favorite grandmother was an inveterate reader. When she was older, she seldom went out, but knew more of world events than the women who constantly attended lectures or club meetings. If a book particularly interested her, she read parts of it aloud, in such an enticing way I could hardly wait to buy it for myself. Any book club would applaud her choices. They included the biblical writings, classics, and poetry along with the modern novel and current-event magazines. If Nannie selected a book as a gift, you knew it was tested and a literary effort to be proud to own.

At the end of the backyard was a garden, which was just as disorganized as the house but full of beauty in a wild way. I found this planting more interesting than my other Grandmother's which, in contrast, was set in precise shapes, filled with prize specimens, a sundial in the middle.

However, Nannie's garden was the product of unexpected gifts and whimsical impulsiveness of the moment. No gift plant was allowed to be dumped before first having its try for perpetuity in the backyard. Often a wilting houseplant managed to thrive in the rich soil of the garden. I think it was encouraged by the casual but loving care of her hands. She would take a shovel, dig an ample hole, and do the planting herself because she didn't want Papa to strain. No edging was attempted but the flowers looked at home in their gay uninhibited bed.

To her, excitement and beauty were everywhere. She made one aware of so much we take for granted. Twilight she considered the most perfect part of the day. Electric lights were not turned on until the last rays of the vanishing day had dissipated. Sitting in peaceful contentment, she watched the quick change of colors in a sunset or the cloud formations of a gathering storm.

The rare eclipse of the sun was an event for which we waited anxiously. Holding the shiny, black negative film, which Nannie provided, we squirmed in suspense for the moment when she would tell us to look through it, right at the sun. There was no letdown, for Nannie told us much of the intricacies of the solar system. It opened up a whole new concept of the universe.

Sometimes we would carry blankets to the yard and all stretch out on our backs. We stared up at the heavens while Nannie described the constellations made up of the diamond like points of light, showing us the Big Dipper, The Southern Cross, and Cassiopeia. We marveled at her knowledge.

Springtime delighted Nannie, and she took us on tramps through the woods and fields, to discover the miracle of nature's wildflowers. The sole kind we were allowed to pick was violets because they would bloom again. Other plants we admired only.

"Some wild flowers have shallow roots or take a long time to grow back," she said. "Also, we want to let others enjoy all this beauty."

In late winter or early spring, Nannie and Papa took us to a maple sugar grove where we saw the sap running into the buckets from the trees. Later, they boiled the syrup and put a little in a saucer. With a spoon, we stirred and stirred the maple syrup until, just as we thought our hands would give out, it miraculously turned creamy white and we had candy. This knack of finding hidden beauty and wonder in everything is a gift I hope I shall never forget.

I was a small, thin child, shy and definitely timid. Once, while staying at Nannie's, some neighborhood children pelted me with snowballs. Unable to defend myself, I ran whimpering to Nannie. That great woman promptly put on hat, coat, and mittens and accompanied me to the enemy territory. I learned much from that incident.

First, she told me one must not run away from disagreeable things. Second, never throw a ball or a snowball like a sissy. Showing me how to throw overhand, she warned me never to deliver such ammunition unless I was prepared to "take it" also. Third, she showed me how to handle myself if an older, bigger group should start picking on me. Instead of futilely trying to fight back, she suggested that I smile and wave a friendly greeting.

Fearfully I tried this method the next time I felt cornered. The unexpectedness of this action so nonplused the older children that after uncertainly waving back, they left me alone.

Nannie was a past master at ego building. I know her education was adequate, but surely included no courses in psychology or psychiatry. Nevertheless, she had developed an unerring instinct for handling people, bringing out the best in a person, making him or her feel important. Once, Grandmother took Nannie, as her companion, on her annual trip to Florida. I sensed that it was not an ideal situation for either party. I'm sure Dad's mother never let the other woman forget that she was deeply indebted to her for the lovely southern trip. I'm equally sure Nannie clamped her lips on any curt retort and acted the part of the grateful recipient.

Rosie was in charge of packing Grandmother's trunk each year, and it was done with precision neatness. Wardrobe trunk was shipped ahead. Black and white dresses were folded carefully with layers of tissue paper between. In the drawers went corset, chemises, hose, and shoes. Jewelry she carried with her in a pouch around her waist.

It was a lengthy trip in those days with a train change at Washington, D.C. On this particular trip, Nannie not only owned no trunk, but also had so few personal belongings, she couldn't have filled one anyway. New acquaintances flocked to Nannie on her visit that year, and she made many close friends. I imagine this irked Grandmother too because she was not glib of tongue, was inept at acting friendly herself.

Because Nannie was so appreciative and such good company, I wanted to do things for her. Once I spent my allowance for reserved seats at a vaudeville show, making the trip downtown by streetcar to purchase the tickets far ahead of time. My choice of guests was Nannie, and she was most enthusiastic. Unfortunately, our seats were in the first row, practically in the orchestra pit, directly by the drummer.

It was disconcerting. At the start of the overture it was almost deafening. I was anxious and worried. However, Nannie assured me they were absolutely the best seats in the house and she would not want any other under any circumstances. I was dubious at first. By constantly praising my astuteness in getting these seats and thanking me prodigiously many times, she was able to convince me I had been clever. This was part of the secret of her success. By the end of the show, I felt warmly pleased that I had accomplished this outing and was eagerly looking forward to the next. It was fun to do things for her because she always seemed genuinely pleased with even the smallest of gestures. A flower was saved, pressed in between the pages of a book, to come upon at a later date and recapture that moment.

Nannie's house was disheveled but comfortable. She did her own housework—sketchily. In the living room was a sagging couch with a bed pillow and blanket for Papa who might want "to stretch out." A dark oak table and chairs dominated the dining room. It was cluttered too, a book of poems, a half-written letter, a dictionary, a scrapbook with clippings yet to go in. She didn't mind interruptions, and the unfinished project just remained where it was abandoned.

Papa loved to tell jokes and stories of the past. His best audience was his wife who, though she must have heard the tales countless times, listened attentively, laughing appreciatively at the proper moment. Papa had played in a band when a boy and loved Sousa music. If he heard a band, he got out the drumsticks and gave us a fancy roll. Nannie was the first to jump into the spirit of it and started us marching around the house which delighted Papa. It didn't seem silly or childish at all because she made it important.

One favorite outing was going to Chardon (on one of those ghastly rides) and gathering chestnuts to bring back to roast over the open fire. I believe the chestnut tree is practically extinct in Ohio but, when I was a child, we went on several of these nut-hunting escapades.

Complete unselfishness is a rare quality. I have never again seen it so well exemplified as in Nannie. She never clung, never reproached, though my visits to the little white house on Cory road sometimes lasted only five minutes.

"Thank you for coming, dear," she said, kissing me.

Gifts were chosen with care and thought. To me, they are now priceless. The clock she gave us for a wedding present has never needed repair. The rocker she used to rock her babies has been used to comfort all four of my children. My most treasured possession is a worn copy of the New Testament. Its pages fall open at the well-read passages she loved. Through it I have learned much of what was important to her.

Youthful ideas and modern inventions make up the world today. Time seems to go faster during these middle years. We cannot and should not try to live in the past, but we do find a source of contentment in reminiscing. Much of the love and wisdom that we gathered in our younger years can be attributed to our elders. I only hope and pray that I am able to pass on to future grandchildren some of the beauty, meaning, and true purpose of life.

2

CHILDREN

We have four children of assorted ages ranging from 33 to 15. How amazing it is that children born to the same parents, theoretically reared the same way, can be so different. Nor can I understand how the mother of four hasn't learned more. Younger mothers used to seek me out for advice, thinking I had the answers and experience. I find the older I get, the less I know.

I feel blessed to have produced four remarkable children. If I had not been able to have my own, I hope I would have adopted. To me, marriage without the experience of raising a family would not be as meaningful.

Granted, children disrupt, interfere, upset our plans, but the majority of us are happier when loved and needed. Love can't be chained or bottled up. The more we give away, the more we receive. This paradox is mystifying but true.

I am appalled at the ignorance of my youth. When I became pregnant with my first child, I was nauseated most of the time, sleepy at ridiculous hours of the day, and didn't know why. Whenever I asked Mother questions, her pat answer was, "I don't remember." Dr. B., the leading obstetrician I visited, was also vague. Apparently he believed the less the prospective mother knew, the better.

Maternity clothes in the thirties were gruesome. Colors were restricted to brown, black or dark green. Style was a uniform wrap around, with ample yardage to accommodate any size. Mother and Grandmother often sighed and said, "A woman is never again as beautiful as with her first baby." This really bothered me, as I didn't think I looked very well. Nor was I sure I had the proper motherly feelings.

When labor started, both John and I became rattled. The cramps were far more severe than we had expected. Excitedly, John called the doctor yelling, "The pains are coming every few minutes!" Dr. B. tired of the calls, let us come on in to the hospital in the middle of the night.

Time dragged endlessly. When the pains became too strong, gas was administered. I slipped back and forth from world to unconsciousness with its accompanying hallucinations. When Bob was born, I was knocked out at the end, too sleepy to appreciate my first sight of him. I recall a tiny purplish face with great masses of long black hair.

Hospital stay was two or three weeks at that time with the maternity floor teeming with help. Trained nurses rubbed your back at night, gave you a complete bed bath in the morning. When homecoming day came, we were apprehensive.

Living in the upper rooms of a double house, the two small bedrooms looked crowded with all the paraphernalia for baby. John and I felt strange with each other, startled when we heard the unfamiliar sucking noises, clucking, and tiny coughs emitting from baby. When Miss K brought him in to nurse in the middle of the night, I felt mature and motherly for the first time.

Karen, our second child, was born three years later. She was reluctant to be born at all. Two and a half weeks overdue, she announced her arrival late at night too.

What the procedure is in other cities, I don't know. Standing at the entrance desk to give your life history while writhing with labor pains was an irritating formality. Expectant mothers may yet be standing in the lobby of maternity hospitals, scared and in pain, clutching the desk as they answer the endless stream of questions. Somehow I don't think so.

John Jr. (Jack) was expected in May. I was entertaining the sewing group the day he arrived. Realizing I should start for the hospital, I relayed the information to one of the girls. All this accomplished was to show me how much preferable it was to have my own comfortable husband, no matter how jittery and irrational he became, to a twittering band of women.

At the hospital, the baby came quickly. When I came to, I had a lovely boy, my husband was there, and I had no voice whatsoever. This disconcerting condition persisted during the entire length of my stay. Dr. B. ranted, scaring the student nurses, sending in throat specialists. No one could satisfactorily explain this loss of voice. Fortunately, the paralysis of the larynx was only temporary.

With mixed emotions, I faced my last pregnancy at age forty. Worrisome to me, it was also a strain on the obstetrician, a lifetime friend. As I waited my turn in his office, I leafed through a magazine. "Chances of a mongoloid baby after forty" was the first article that came to my attention.

Despite attempts to dwell on pleasant thoughts, doubts crept in. Even the doctor was cautious, making my appointments more frequent.

After the initial shock of realization that I actually was having this baby, I was delighted, feeling unique. The reaction of friends was interesting. Some were embarrassed, thinking it was indecent of me to beget at this age. One dear neighbor was frankly horrified; others were wistful. The younger generation eyed me in a new light too. At home, Bob's friends were solicitous, jumping to their feet to help me across the room, plumping pillows behind my back, generally treating me gingerly.

We made a trip to New York when I was in the sixth month. What a gratifying revelation to know there were still gentlemanly souls who leapt to their feet to offer me a seat on the bus. One man even relinquished his taxi to me. Truly I felt like a queen. As the time of birth neared, I was more and more miserable physically. I was so very tired. Fervently I agreed with God's and Nature's plan for only the young to reproduce.

Pam came early. John was just as nervous and jittery as the first time. I begged him to drive slower, but he was in terror I might have the baby in the car. Frankly, I was too! The hospital was a welcome sight.

Maternity was a weird contrast from my first introduction. Not only was there a frightening shortage of nurses but also, arriving ahead of schedule, I didn't have a room either.

Both my husband and I had wanted another girl. Neither of us had dared express aloud our wish. It was enough to pray for a normal child. When the doctor said, "You have a lovely baby girl," I couldn't believe it and said so. Whereupon, he lifted her up, cord still attached, so I could see for myself. Though premature, no incubator was needed. What a thrill to be awake for the birth of this healthy girl.

With the scarcity of nurses and no room, I felt neglected. First, I asked for some breakfast. None appeared. Next, I inquired about a bedpan. No one had one of those either. Finally, I got out of bed, wandered down the hall until I found a bathroom. Wistfully I thought of those back rubs and bed baths of another era. After the third day, my pediatrician advised me to go home. "You are not getting any rest, the baby is fine, and you are fine. Why not go home and sleep?" That is exactly what I did.

There is a theory, the folk wisdom of many countries condensed into a saying that gifted children inherit from their grandparents, so that talents skip a generation. Bob's grandfather was a study in meticulousness. Perhaps that is why Bob is so neat. Heredity should be considered. Of equal importance, however, is environment.

Certainly whether consciously or subconsciously the way we were brought up reflects in the way we raise our own children. Because Mother was so trusting, I think I felt the same way. I did not wait up for my children. Usually I heard them anyway without sitting up like a guard.

If it was very late, they sneaked in, just as I used to. I learned to avoid two squeaky stairs, but I know Mother heard me. Dad was a sound sleeper. If Mother worried, she kept it to herself to protect me from Dad's wrath. He had no patience with late hours. However the attitude of trust worked. If one expects the best of others, perhaps that is what they will receive.

I know one mother who was so suspicious of her son, she accused him of everything from drink to drugs. She relayed the constant nagging and lack of trust to the father who was seldom home. One night, the boy got hold of a gun, shot his father and wounded his mother. I think he meant to kill the mother. This is an extreme example. Maybe a little love and trust would have resulted in a different story.

Fortunately or unfortunately the example you set may be the one your child follows. How can I fuss at a youngster for a fault of which I am guilty myself? Sometimes I think they benefit from our bad points too. I was a compulsive smoker for many years. This dirty habit repulsed all the children who vowed never to start. This was particularly true after they witnessed my first unsuccessful attempt to quit.

One of the commonest faults of parents is the urge to mold the child to the unreal, idealistic image you want him or her to be. Now that my four children are grown up, at least in years, it is interesting to reflect on how many early traits they have retained, what influence parents, grandparents, and environment had on them.

Our eldest son, Bob, has achieved an assistant professorship at a western university. He's become an author, researcher, administrator, and world traveler. In his earlier days, no one could have prophesied these accomplishments. Specific personality traits, however, hinted at the possibility of success.

For example, he displayed a remarkable ability to organize his young life. Though only a toddler, he safeguarded his toys by neatly returning them to his cupboard at naptime. Bob frequently demonstrated his affinity for neatness. On one occasion, I planted lima beans in our country garden. I finished a row and turned around, there was Bob toddling behind me. Over his left arm he held a basket. With his right hand, he was conscientiously picking up each bean from its freshly dug trench.

Bob's terrific determination was apparent from the first gusty cry to now. When he learned to crawl, he crept for miles, developing leathery knees and strong legs, curious about all his surroundings. Walking was the same. There was no fumbling.

First, he practiced in the playpen, raising and lowering himself methodically. Next, he tiptoed around the perimeter, hanging on to the edge of the pen. When he decided he had learned the elementary sufficiently, he just took off. Instead of observing and recording Baby's first step alone, it was more like recording Baby's first hike!

This energetic persistence has continued. Such driving force to go forward has helped him to accomplish much. His love of work and play was well balanced when he was young. I felt close to him as most mothers do with their first-born son. If he has gained success today, it is mostly through his own gigantic efforts, his tireless self-discipline.

However, I believe parents contribute much to the success of a child, whether by conscious effort or by the example they set. I well remember the constant coaching of manners, "Stand up for a lady," "Take off your hat in an elevator," "Hold a chair for your grandmother," "Hold the door for your elders." Just when it seemed a waste of breath to repeat once more, an occasion would arise where I would stand gaping at my son performing all the niceties I had despaired of his ever remembering.

Bob was born in the depression of the thirties. John and I scrimped to send the boy to private school, college, and graduate school. Today, a teacher, he is the proud possessor of seven degrees, including a Ph.D. How did he happen to choose this profession? Because he had shared in material possessions, they became meaningless to him. Success to him meant his personal contribution to society, not monetary gains. I'm sure my husband had dreamed of both sons joining the family business. Neither did.

Even while young, Bob was a contradiction of many things. Shy, soft-spoken, he was at the same time friendly with a warm wonderful smile. Recognizing the handicap of shyness, he forced himself to try to conquer it. At age five, when he offered to make a purchase for me, I let him. Cheeks aflame, money clutched tightly in his small fist, he marched into the village store. In a quivering voice he asked for a quart of ice cream. It was one of countless hurdles he forced himself to overcome.

Bob displayed a serious attitude about his work. But he captivated strangers with his contagious laugh. Though he learned to swim, his style was wild and thrashing. Strong and competitive, he stubbornly rejected the idea of lessons. Then one day Bob lost a race. He began to realize that sheer will to win was not enough. Skill and training mattered too. Recognizing this, he worked persistently, resulting in eight athletic letters in high school and a new record at the swim club.

When Bob was a freshman in high school, he fell in love for the first time with a mature eighth grader. I worried about her aggressiveness, sensing Bob would not be able to keep up with her. Soon, she became very popular. Though Bob held on for a while, he could not match her pace and lost her to some one else.

It was a bad year for him. Nothing quite went right. "Thy will be done," I kept saying to myself. After he recovered sufficiently from this first love affair, he went with Jane. Through high school and college they dated. Break-off time came when Bob made the major decision of his life, which was to go west to start a lengthy program of graduate work. Again the fading of love affected me. No doubt a mother should not feel so deeply.

Athletics were stressed at the high school where eventually our son won the award for the best all-around athlete. He earned it through hard work and strict training rules of his own making.

Weak eyes necessitated glasses. For this reason, the coach tried to discourage him from baseball, his favorite sport. Stubbornly, Bob decided he was going to play baseball and try to become captain of the team, regardless of obstacles. Accordingly we bought him shatterproof glasses.

My heart ached for him those high school years. I thought his goal an impossible one. Joining a sandlot team, he rode his small motorcycle many miles to practice night after night. In his senior year he was elected captain of the baseball team, received his letter and the satisfaction of knowing he had accomplished what he set out to do. That ended the baseball career. To my knowledge he has never played since.

For a fall sport, he played soccer. His level headedness proved valuable in the games. Though not the spectacular type, he was an asset to the team in high school and during his four years at college.

Bob exemplified the wisdom of words softly spoken. A mild suggestion from him produced more action than the angry command of a more belligerent individual. His brother Jack, seven years his junior was irresponsible and careless at the time. Suddenly, I realized he was serving his brother like a personal valet, even shining his shoes. I'm sure Jack was bewildered by the subtle way this state of being had come to pass. Similar techniques were applied to Mom.

Putting his arm around me Bob murmured affectionately, "Are you going to make some of your wonderful date bars, Mom?" The only difference in this approach was that I knew darn well he was "buttering" me. I was just as flattered. Actually, it was fun to cook for this first-born son because he devoured all homemade cooking. We called him our human disposal. He couldn't stand to see a lone chop or a slice of cake return to the kitchen. No worries about leftovers when he was home!

Whether plowing the garden or moving furniture, Bob performed cheerfully any menial chore I exacted. I tried to instill in all my children the trait of giving a helping hand. Each was required to make his bed, empty wastebaskets, and help with the dishes or yard work. In all fairness, I must say all four did these things, but some more amiably than others.

Bob always found a summer job. From his swimming experience, he obtained a job as lifeguard at one of the area's club pool. His patience and quiet calm encouraged his pupils. Commanding the respect of the pool swimmers, he never had to blow his whistle for discipline, kept it for emergency messages only.

One trait that endeared Bob to me was his complete lack of self-consciousness with Mother. He always kissed me goodnight, a casual display of good-natured affection that in no way embarrassed him at any age. Our youngest boy, on the other hand, went through a difficult period in his maturing where he preferred to ignore family, especially parents. In fact, if there had been any way to delete them from his life, he would have been happier.

Bob, however, seemed to slide from little boy to manhood with scarcely a ripple. Perhaps because he was so dependable, I expected more of him and treated him as an adult. I don't know. Strange that the problems one usually encounters with a first born, just didn't exist in this case. I can only conclude that my youth, instinct, and ignorance were a better formula than age and experience.

Bob is basically frugal. Once, when the whole family was on an extended vacation, the crisp, five-dollar bill he carried for frivolities, returned home with him intact. If we needed a nickel or dime, we went elsewhere.

After college Bob spent two years at a top university in California, earning a degree at business school. At entrance time, he had no place to live. Spending the first few nights at the western chapter of his fraternity, he became known. Shortly thereafter, the class dean accepted him as house advisor and fraternity chaperone. Again this offered opportunity to associate with people, learning to guide, talk, and offer advice from his own limited experiences.

His graduate work required long hours of study that were constantly interrupted by the undergraduate student problems. Living quarters under the stairway were like living in the hall, easily accessible, never quiet. For this service, he received room and board. Paying for this in shorter sleep time, no privacy, it is astounding he could do so well. Concentration under all circumstances has been one of his most valued accomplishments.

Bestowal of a business school degree was only the beginning. Between semesters one summer, he traveled extensively in Latin America, visiting every country there. From the time he left California by bus to Mexico and south, he forced himself not to speak one word of English. Intrigued by this young man's earnest endeavor to learn the language of the country, whether Spanish or Portuguese, many paused to help him, to correct his speech. Traveling alone, he met many natives who welcomed him in their homes, sharing their meager table fare. As a result of this trip, he became passionately interested in South American affairs. Pursuing this field at the conclusion of business school, he went to Spain and Portugal for two years. The Brazilian Portuguese he had learned differed sharply from the language spoken in Lisbon. Doggedly, he continued struggling with the different pronunciations. Soon after, he collected a degree from the University of Lisbon and then from the University of Madrid.

Ultimately, each one of us must conquer our own weaknesses. A mother can help to some extent. By pushing Bob a trifle, he gained the impetus to get over some of his reserve and timidity. Consistent, honest praise for work well done, can build confidence.

Today, I worry about this eldest son, though he is married, a father with two sons of his own. World traveler, author, and speaker, he is held in high esteem, not only at the university where he teaches, but also in the outreach circles of his field. But, with all this knowledge, I feel he lives too in a tight, limited world. I feel helpless to alleviate it. He has disciplined himself to use every precious minute to attain the high goals he has set for himself. Thus, he allows little time for frivolity, relaxation, and pure fun.

Our first-born was a favorite with my dad who stopped often to see the boy and play with him. Through my dad, Bob learned the intricacies of telling time, the mastering of the dial phone, and much of how to read. They remained great friends. Each respected the other's accomplishments. Dad attended many of the high school soccer games, braving the icy winds to watch Bob play. When my parents came to Dartmouth to see Bob graduate, it was one of the proudest moments in Dad's life. At Bob's out-of-town wedding, his grandfather was too ill to attend, and the moment the ceremony was over, before the receiving line began, the new groom voluntarily raced to the phone to call my father long distance.

Substituting grandson for the son he never had, Dad found the relationship satisfying. Likewise, Bob revered the knowledge, the wisdom that years of experience had taught his grandfather. Maybe it is a common occurrence. To me, as an observer, it was beautiful. I am grateful.

From the time she was born, Karen was a charmer, as feminine as Bob was boyish. With her arrival came a whole new set of problems. At naptime, she spent the two hours taking apart her crib, eating cold cream or finger painting on the furniture with powder, water or whatever was handy.

I went through this routine daily, thinking the solitude would be restful. Usually it was more disastrous than beneficial. When I questioned the doctor on some of her strange habits, he reminded me I had just been lucky having an easy first baby, that I didn't know how to cope with more average riddles.

Karen was smart, learning to read before she went to school. First grade bored her. She did well in school, but it was book learning. Dates of ancient history were memorized. Curiosity about the world today was lacking. At adolescence there appeared to be a great rapport between her and her father.

When she was thirteen, she retired to her room, reading and writing poetry, shunning the outside world. If her father admonished her mildly, she dissolved into tears, leaving her dad bewildered and frustrated. She was pretty with delicate pink coloring that intensified with excitement or shyness. A good athlete, she had instruction in all sports and excelled in most of them. Nonetheless, for many years she resented her older brother and his ability. Also, she was bitter over any mention of others' athletic prowess. When her father admired a classmate, Mary, and her excellent horsemanship, Karen construed this to mean it was criticism of herself. Horses became a true enemy. Was it super-sensitivity? Was it a concealed desire to please father? In retrospect, life takes on a different complexion.

Going away to camp would have benefited her, but the mere thought sickened her. Whenever a camp director learned of her reluctance to leave the comfort of home, they advised me to reject camp altogether. She worried about me in her younger years. Everyone drank too much, stayed up too late, many impromptu parties evolved. Once she told me that she used to rock herself to sleep chanting, "Mommie doesn't love me, Mommie doesn't love me." This horrified me and still haunts me!

Could we do a better job if given a second chance? I doubt it. Certainly we can change, but it is nigh impossible to live another's life. Karen was popular. But, with one or two exceptions, she remained aloof, afraid to express herself or show any genuine warmth for anyone outside the family.

Perhaps boys are more organized than girls, dirtier, but not so sloppy. Whenever I admonished Karen about the condition of her room, she grumbled, flounced, but in the end, "cleaned it up." From a hasty scanning, it looked neat, feminine, until you realized that only a miracle could have changed that chaos to order in such a short time. Further perusal showed piles of books, papers, and stockings stashed under the bed. All superfluous clothes landed down the clothes chute.

When Karen was invited to her first school prom, we suddenly faced the problem of what to wear. On this I decided to give her full rein. Horrifying memories of my first school dance wafted over me.

I recalled the shame I felt for being with a younger boy which necessitated parents driving. Noting the older girls with hair crimped and marcelled, quickly, I discarded the barrette, which left my hair hanging over one eye in what I thought was a provocative manner. Instead it looked like I had forgotten to put on the fastener.

Mother blithely ignored all signals of physical maturing. I was faced with the problem of how to banish the wispy hairs in the armpit. The boyish flat front was the style of the day, and therefore, the fact that I was not yet very developed did not concern me. I didn't have a fantastic time, but I learned a lot. I carefully stored away all the tricks of makeup, action, and dress that I observed on the older girls.

As our children grew up, I recalled all those things. When I let Karen decide on her attire, I thought I was being exceptionally astute. She was definite about the kind of dress she wanted. It was to be a long blue net, sleeveless gown. This didn't sound too difficult. After school one day and on Saturdays, we shopped casually at the suburban centers. Later, frantically at the downtown stores, we visited every department in every store, including the bargain basement—not a long blue dress anywhere. In the end, Karen chose a waltz-length aqua dress, which we could have bought the first day.

Again, if I had behaved like most mothers, I would have refused to spend those endless hours looking for a non-existent formal. Did I spoil her by catering to her whims? Or by my own memories, was I showing understanding? At the time, the choice of the dress seemed vitally important to me to instill confidence in herself.

Because she had never been away from home, Karen's departure for college was a real wrench for everyone. Later, she confided she had cried all night on the train getting there.

Despite stormy sessions and misunderstandings, we were a close family. People envied us. I was accused by husband and friends of devoting too much time to children. We survived many heartaches, illnesses, and traumatic experiences.

Karen hated college but refused to transfer or drop out. Our phone bills were our costliest service those days. During her junior years, she lost much weight, couldn't sleep, and worked like a fiend. She was on a dizzying circle. Before

Christmas our family doctor and friend advised us to get her home as soon as possible. After exams, she continued her studies locally seemingly content to live at home.

Senior year she returned to her class in the eastern college. Very soon she became enmeshed with a young man working in New York. At Thanksgiving, I invited him and his mother to visit. Suddenly, my husband had urgent business on the west coast. I have secretly questioned the necessity of that trip. At any rate, he abandoned me to the whole weekend—and what a weekend it was!

We survived Thanksgiving Day, each mother bragging of her child. When we retired for the night, I cautioned the young couple to make sure the flame was out in the fireplace. Karen had given up her room to the future mother-in-law, was bunking with me. I awakened when she came to bed. After ten minutes of listening to her toss, I dozed off, only to be awakened by Karen squealing, "I think the house is on fire."

I couldn't smell any smoke. After telling her to call the fire department, my next thought was to get dressed. In sub zero weather I should be properly clothed, I reasoned. That notion was quickly dropped. As I pulled the nightgown over my head, I heard the roar of fire, wood crackling in the walls behind where I was changing. Grabbing a coat, I raced from room to room, waking the occupants.

No one reacted quickly enough. Pammy, aged five, started to cry. I yanked her to her feet, telling her there was no time for tears. Our houseguest wanted to pack and take the curlers from her hair. I had a hard time with her. Jack decided to play hero. Dragging on his pants as he raced down stairs, he ran for the fire extinguisher. By this time, smoke was seeping into the living room, a horrible greenish-black mess.

Suddenly I realized the danger of fumes. Cordelia, the massive cook, wanted to go back for her false teeth. Somehow I was able to dissuade her. Now everyone was out except Jack. Hoping to oust him, I screamed, "The cars! They will catch on fire. Help me get them out." This made sense to the young teenager, so he left.

One last look and I saw the flames leaping out by the fireplace, latching on to the curtains and the lampshade. By the time we got to the street, a lively blaze was raging in the house. I didn't feel any emotion but relief. Everyone was out! Neighbors arrived, patting me, and make consoling noises.

As I watched the fire, I thought how meaningless are the material things in life. The house we had worked so hard to build was being destroyed in front of my eyes. I didn't even care. I felt proud that no one had dashed in for a foolish rescue. Everyone was safe. That was all that mattered.

Memories of that night are jumbled. I can't believe it all happened. Many of our friends were away for the holiday weekend, but neighbors came to the scene and divided us up—Jack and the dog at one house, Cordelia at another, Karen at her girlfriend's, Pammy, house guest, and I two doors away. Firemen put out the fire. Then it was up to me to check. I toured every inch of the house, closing windows.

Eyeing the damage unemotionally, it was impossible to assess. The roof was intact. Although the living room was gutted, the room above it charred, the furnace was still functioning. I noticed a sticky, brown coating on everything, but didn't know the serious consequences of smoke damage.

Karen had an eight o'clock morning appointment to have a wisdom tooth extracted. For some inane reason, it didn't occur to either of us to cancel it, though we had been awake all night. Karen and I arrived at the dentist office far too early. They would have been happier if we had cancelled. Apparently our clothes, hair, and our very bodies smelled of smoke. In fact, it was weeks before we were really free of it. Even shoes carried the odor.

Everyone wanted to go back to the ill-fated house, including Sam, the fiancée, who decided to play protector. Not his mother, though. She had had enough! We were all jumpy. No one wanted to be alone so we moved mattresses and beds.

We did sleep, more or less huddled in dormitory fashion. One of John's more casual friends came over. Even he paled visibly when he viewed the disaster, which he promptly nicknamed "The Embers." Finally, against my wishes he felt obligated to phone my husband in California to report on "the little fire." When John did arrive home, he was aghast at the sight, appalled that we were still living at home. It was stupid on my part. Let me assure you, one doesn't always do the rational thing when your house is on fire.

Temporary housing was at the country club where Pam and I were sick for a while from smoke inhalation. Nighttime was the worst. Invariably we thought we smelled smoke. To this day, Karen cannot bear the sound of a fire siren. I was determined that Christmas would not be spoiled. Bob came home from business school in California, Karen from college in the east. We dragged a tree up to our room, trimmed and decorated it. Probably we felt closer as a family that year than at any other time, thankful to be alive, grateful to be together.

To describe the amount of work involved in a house fire is difficult. Extent of damage was not apparent at first. Fortunately, John is the type who keeps records, with data on original cost, dates, and so on. Many fools commented to me, "How lucky you are to get everything new!" On a twenty thousand dollar fire (much more at today's prices) let me assure you it's a battle every inch of the way.

Insurance companies are fair, I'm sure, but one must have proof of loss. For example, we had just redecorated our bedroom. Because the furniture had left the store, been installed in the home, the merchandise was no longer new. Therefore you take a loss. To replace carpeting of the same quality of the living room cost far more than the adjustor would allow.

Nylon lingerie that had been in a drawer, all had a brown smoke streak across the fold. I washed, I bleached, and I soaked. Nothing would remove the stains. Another claim, but can you remember when you bought each article of underwear? John and I walked around with notebooks under our arms at all times. Each evening, we went over figures. One definite benefit from this fire was that it improved my arithmetic. I felt like an adding machine, keeping charts, and prices of daily living expenses too.

As soon as carpenters and painters were through and utilities in working order, we moved back to the house. However, it was many months before we finished.

Karen and Sam announced their engagement at Christmas despite my entreaties to wait until June and graduation. To return to college with a diamond on her finger was important to her. Looking back, maybe she was just in love with the idea of love. I went ahead with the plans, reserving church and minister for an August wedding.

In late spring, we discovered our daughter had many doubts about the forthcoming marriage and was going ahead with it because she thought it was too late to change. We put an immediate halt to everything. Difficult moments resulted. The rejected suitor insisted on attending her graduation, which made it awkward for all of us. Karen behaved abominably towards him.

With the engagement broken, Karen away, the bulk of the problems fell on me. Sam had been living at our house while he was traveling and had become rather attached to me. He appeared often, wanting to talk. John disappeared, muttering excuses of deskwork. There I was, at the mercy of Sam and his frustration. He had adopted the idea that this was a temporary postponement, a phase every girl went through.

Eventually, after many such midnight talks, I told him, as gently as possible that, in my estimation, Karen was not going to marry him and the sooner he found a new young lady, the better. It was a painful experience, but it seemed best to avoid holding out hope. I knew my daughter. Actually, during that upheaval period, communication between parents and daughter were at a high level.

Today, Karen is a sophisticated young matron of thirty, married (to someone else) and mother of a four-year-old boy. With money no issue, she has settled into a life of volunteer work, suburbia, and country clubs. Busy with committees, she heads many of them. She and her husband lead an active social life. At the same time, Karen is a good mother.

However, I worry about her too. Will she ever relax and again see the beauty in simple pleasures? The poetry she once composed lies neglected. Beautiful, thought-provoking lines are buried. At my urging, she submitted some poems to a magazine but accepted defeat with the first rejection slip. As any author knows, the first hurdle to jump is sensitivity on refusals. Perhaps one day she will return to this and share her gift of beauty with others.

Jack is a tough, two-hundred-pound Marine captain, so muscular that he never looks well groomed in ready-made suits. His thighs strain at the pant leg. As a child, he never looked neat, regardless of all the scrubbing, brushing, and shining. He, clothes, and I had a struggle always.

The first battle with clothes occurred when he was still a toddler, using the dresser drawers as ladder rungs to reach the top. Along the way, he rid himself of the superfluous. Piles of clean garments were shuffled with the soiled, the whole lot thrown down the clothes chute. I scolded, I spanked, and I pleaded—to no avail. Finally I removed all wearing apparel and furniture from his room. The sole object in the room was the crib.

As soon as he was old enough to dress himself, he chose outfits at random, completely ignoring practicality, weather conditions, color, or any of the factors that ordinarily trigger our decisions. A hot summer day might find him in a long sleeved-turtle neck. On a cold, windy one he might appear in a sun suit. Later, if I didn't stay alert, he might start for dancing school with his dark blue suit on, but worn with dirty white track shoes. Still later, I once caught him wearing his tuxedo shirt over a numeraled tee shirt so that the number twenty-seven showed through.

He was impulsive, annoying, obstreperous but very imaginative. Teachers and neighbors became irritated. In sympathy with a teacher's frustration, I spent much time trying to explain my son to them. Jack was smart but accomplished only average grades with poor marks on effort. Unless he was truly interested, he didn't bother. I'm sure this is what distressed the teachers. They suspected it was partially their fault for not rousing enough stimulation.

"Accident prone kid" was an apt nomenclature for Jack. Whenever I arrived at school to pick him up if he was not visible, I knew he was either at the principal's office or in the infirmary. Twice we rushed him to the emergency entrance of the hospital when he was found unconscious by his bicycle.

Either he felt the dearth of boys his age in our neighborhood or maybe he just felt unloved. Whatever the reason, he deemed it necessary to rely on a group of imaginary friends. Ghost, Burglar and Snake were his favorites. They remained with us for quite a while. Sometimes it required a deft explanation to convince people that this second son was not some kind of a nut. A tougher mother would have squashed such nonsense at its conception.

I could understand it was reassuring to him. Hadn't I had my own support, my lucky elephant? Most of us have some sort of security blanket, whether it is a baby toy too cherished to discard, or a childish habit of rocking, doodling by the phone. At least it shows imagination. How dull to live in a complete world of reality.

Jack was a collector. First it was rocks. His pockets, corners of the room were filled with an assortment of stones. Next dawned the butterfly era. This was not a momentary hobby, but a long study. Once, when he was eleven we took a trip to New York City. One of the highlights for him was visiting a little shop which was exclusively for butterfly collectors. We bought one or two rare specimens.

Our younger son always showed a tremendous amount of courage, physically and mentally. When he was about eight, his older brother and a friend dared him to do a back dive into the lake. As he didn't know how to go headfirst either, he decided backwards couldn't be any harder. To the amazement of the two older boys, he marched out to the end of the board, turned, balanced, and executed a fairly successful back dive.

Slaloming on water skis the first time out, Jack maneuvered the course around the lake through sheer strength and bravado. In college boards, he took the advanced math examination, though he had not yet been taught some of the material.

At soccer, he tried out for the most challenging position on the team. In diving competition, he worked on the intricate dives, the ones with the highest degree of difficulty. Perfection at a lower level did not satisfy him. Always the toughest course was the best in his thinking.

As far as I know, my children were truthful, at least on the important issues. I admired my younger boy who managed to get into the most serious scrapes. If it was bad, he plowed right into the confession quickly. I think he was often equally surprised that we could be human, ready to support him in time of trouble.

Once, he turned over in his car. It was not the first accident either. Rolled down an embankment, the car was almost demolished. Miraculously he came out in one piece, with only minor wounds and abrasions. He phoned his dad telling him exactly what had happened, how it occurred, and the extent of the damage.

I was very proud of my husband this time. He didn't raise his voice. Although his hand holding the phone was shaking, he remained calm, telling Jack precisely what to do, praising him for his skill in emerging alive. Moments like this I hope are remembered. If they are ignored now, I'm sure when similar situations arise with their children, they will recall these exquisite feelings of understanding.

Sometimes I wonder if it is wise to remember so well. Maybe I would be a better mother if I could think more like a parent. In a given situation or minor clash with a teenager, I recall so vividly how I myself felt at that age. Then it is difficult to be sensible and motherly. My habit of lying down with my feet up on the wall was probably worse than the barefoot mode of today. At least the feet unusually are on the floor where they belong.

I don't like the freakish dress of some of the young. On the other hand, I get irritated with the oldsters who brand all outrageously dressed kids as hippies.

Music is a vital link in communication with the young. I have always felt most popular music, whether blues, jazz, country western or whatever, is immensely sad. When I was young, I used to hang over the Victrola, memorizing words of the current song. One can identify with a song that otherwise might sound absurd if spoken aloud. Cab Calloway was one of my favorites. It drove Dad wild to hear that constant caterwauling that made Cab famous.

Today's music is no different. With radios, it is more continuous, with a push of the button, and we have music. Some of the songs today, if you listen carefully, are truly sad, great pleas for help. Youngsters feel and experience through music what they cannot express otherwise.

When our young son was home, Chuck Berry and Johnny Rivers were bellowing on the Hi-Fi. I thought of Dad and his abhorrence of Cab. When Jack left for college, I found the abrupt silence unbearable. One morning, feeling like a traitor, I put on a stack of records, which he had left home. Only then did I feel right with the world.

Jack's struggle for direction was a long one. In high school he was erratic in his academic standing, depending on the interest or teacher. Languages appealed to him. Becoming absorbed in the fascination of physics, suddenly involved all of his time. No one was more surprised than Jack when his French marks went tumbling down. A leveling period was slow in coming.

At first, every guest speaker who talked in assembly period at school stressed the tremendous expected enrollment of college students by 1960, a result of the growing up of the "war babies." "By 1960 only the top student will get accepted at college" was the ominous prediction.

Theoretically, this warning was to stir up the lazy scholar, inspire him to work harder. With Jack, it worked in reverse. "If only A students will get in anyway, why work?" he reasoned. Not until senior year did he become motivated enough to live up to the potential I knew he had. His extremely high score in French helped his admittance to the college of his choice.

Like many of us, Jack was unsure of himself, covering up his lack of confidence by a display of bravado, which the less observant might mistake for cockiness. Freshman year at college, he signed up for NROTC with a surging enthusiasm for the Navy. The following year, a persuasive recruiter must have relayed the proper message for he switched to the Marine Corps.

Before he made his decision, he phoned us seeking advice. This was one of those moments in life when the answer you give may be the most important of a son's career. We did not know nor did we want to give the answer. I knew it involved three years of active service after four years of college. I suggested, weakly, that the Navy cruise (required junior year) was a chance to see the world.

With his usual hard-road route, Jack said it was too soft a life. The Marine Corps was more challenging. Right or wrong, Jack made his decision and chose the U.S.M.C. Later, when he was in battle, we thought of that phone call. If we had attempted to sway him, would events have differed?

During his junior year, Jack invited us to be resident chaperones at spring house parties. I accepted with alacrity. Perhaps he thought we would decline or perhaps he wanted us to tote his girl of the moment. She was a voluptuous blonde who sat in silence for most of the motor trip there. Whenever I tried to engage her in conversation, she responded in a monosyllable, polite enough, but leaving no opening to continue. Eventually I gave up. She was relieved. Feigning sleep to avoid further small talk, Seline kept her eyes closed the rest of the journey.

Jack greeted us with misgivings, I'm sure. Our room was directly over the spot where the band played for dancing. Fortunately there was a lock on the door, which I learned to use after several couples wandered in seeking privacy. I tired to assure our son that we had been young once and had lived through some pretty wild times. However, I could see he was dubious. Having given us his warnings of possible indiscretions, he wondered off, and we were left on our own.

As far as I could see, males and females behaved much in the same manner as girls and boys in our day. The main difference was the unembarrassment of group action. According to college rules, resident chaperones were to be visible until the close of the party (about four in the morning). The din of the band, the wildness of the dance performed in bare feet on a beer sodden floor, finally got to us. No one was on the main floor. We made ourselves comfortable in easy chairs, settled down to watch the late, late movie on television.

After a half hour, I poked my husband to turn around and see the couples who had quietly joined us, not for watching TV however. As far as they were concerned, we were just part of the fixed furnishings in the room. Uncertain as to what to do, we did nothing. Boys themselves had their own code of ethics, wanting no trouble from the authorities. No women above the first floor, no obnoxious drunks. A policeman stood at the door, presumably to discourage unwelcome visitors.

With the resiliency of youth, everyone was back by eleven the next morning for brunch, drinks, and dancing. Jack eyed us reflectively but made no comment. It was an experience I wouldn't have missed. I feel flattered to have been asked whatever the reason. With today's freedom, probably a chaperone is classified along with other antiques.

Seline managed to look sexy all weekend. I never heard her talk much. I guess she didn't need to. She didn't return with us, which caused a stir with her sister and the college she attended. Apparently she had signed out for one night only. Her parents were divorced. Neither one was interested in her whereabouts. I hope it got straightened out. I did not hear the sequel.

Just before graduation, Jack was involved in a foolish motorcycle accident whereby he received a serious leg injury. Hospitalized, he was treated and released, only to have the infection flare up later. His leg swelled to painful proportions. None of this did we know of course until he called us from the hospital. Anxiously conferring with the attending physician, we learned it was truly blood poisoning. If he did not respond to the penicillin, he was in danger of losing his leg.

Frantic calls ensued. When we arrived on campus for graduation ceremonies, our boy was weak, pale, and on crutches. A doctor's excuse released him from rehearsal, but he hobbled along on a cane anyway. How he managed graduation day itself, I don't know. It must have been painful.

The Marine Corps allowed him an extra year to complete his studies, earning an engineering degree. It was a proud moment when I pinned his lieutenant bars on his dress whites at the commissioning, an impressive display.

When Jack joined the Marines, I believe I had a premonition of things to come. As we often do, I postponed worrying about it at the time. I knew he wanted the chance to prove himself in a tough environment. After the commissioning ceremony, I realized that the esprit de corps had already been instilled in him.

That first summer at Quantico, he wrote with gusto expressing great enthusiasm after six weeks of intensive training. Even the eighteen-hour day did not dampen his spirits. Each new phase was challenging. There was instruction on map reading, intelligence, use of field radios, weapons, and platoon and squad tactics.

This was followed by many hours of practical applications in the field. His letters were eager. As I suspected, he wrote that he had put in for duty in Viet Nam. Since he had finished second out of three hundred eighty-five for the first ten weeks, he was assured of his choice of duty station.

As the possibility of his participation in the war in Viet Nam became more and more of a reality, I could see that Jack was driven by a passion to see life at its best and worst. He felt desperately the need to become more self-reliant, to possess more self-esteem.

To date, his life had been too easy, secure, with few tough obstacles to surmount. But obviously there was more. I wondered how much he knew of the Vietnamese people, their lives, and dreams of their trials. Was it a personal compulsion to Jack, or a call to arms? Little patriotism was shown anywhere in this undeclared war in South Viet Nam.

To me, Viet Nam meant a small lush country stretching S-shaped twelve hundred miles. It had always been a far-away land, completely divorced from anything pertaining to our own world. Now, suddenly, this tiny country was of vital importance.

Most of the history, I gleaned from books of Bernard Fall, the leading historian on affairs of South East Asia. He had carefully documented the Viet Nam struggle with the French. Now we were face-to-face with vicious battle ourselves. I had heard of how Diem had oppressed the people and how they had finally overthrown him. I was unaware of the scope and magnitude of the massive buildup, the scale of the war then taking place.

On November 29, 1965, Jack called to say he had received his orders directing him to West Pacific ground forces on January 24. He wrote that night; "I must admit I found myself shaking at the reality. Only twelve of the three hundred eighty-five men are being sent directly over as platoon commanders. When I called, I could tell you were upset. Have faith. It's what I want." I had immeasurable faith in Jack; it was the Viet Cong I didn't trust. From that moment on, life took on a completely new complexion. I was scared. I didn't convey that to Jack; it was a vital, necessary step to make his future more meaningful and directed.

The uncertainty, the shelter of childhood, the indecisions of what route to take must all be shed before this acceptance of himself as a man could be realized. Some of us have a compelling drive to follow the intuitive feeling of what is best for our lives. Sometimes this is not the safest or easiest path.

Jack's orders changed to report to Camp Pendleton in California for an undetermined amount of time. When he showed a desire to have his car out on the west coast, I suggested hesitantly that I help him drive it out. To my surprised, he did not laugh at me. "Sure," he said. "Why not?"

Why not indeed! I had a hundred reasons why I should not leave at that particular time. Also I had a sick feeling at the pit of my stomach warning me I might never see him again.

For a short while, it was one of the best things I have ever done. We drove long hours at first, reaching Albuquerque the second night, a long haul from our Midwestern home. Far enough west, we felt sufficiently secure to do a little detouring. Consequently, we went to the Painted Desert, down the Salt River Canyon in a snowstorm to Tucson. One night we spent in Las Vegas, which was not on our route at all.

In California, Jack proceeded to Camp Pendleton. I left for Arizona. No sooner had I arrived there than Jack called to say his orders had been changed again. One more leave before going overseas. In a panic, I called home urging my husband to leave sooner and meet us in California. After many expensive calls, we made our plans. John flew to the coast, I flew from Arizona, and we had the weekend with Jack.

On Sunday, we drove to Camp Pendleton. Raining steadily, bleak and cold, the weather contributed to our already sodden spirits. When we left the lonely lieutenant standing in the rain outside his barracks, the tears were running down both our faces. "Would we ever see him again?" Two weeks later he left for Vietnam.

With Jack's absence, life at home changed significantly. Each news report was followed intensely. In fact, the dinner hour was switched so there was time to get the visual action on television. At times it was difficult to control emotions and imagination. If I heard of any Marine encounter, it was a natural assumption that Jack was a part of it. Of course, I had no way of knowing. By the time he wrote of an incident, I was busy worrying about another current one.

Jack sent home a box of mementos, which I opened. I spread out the content to dry for the papers were still soggy and covered with mildew from the steaming jungle. In a notebook, I found some passages that showed how quickly and dramatically Jack was thrust into the ugly war. How different from the training to find one's self face-to-face with the real thing. An entry of February 27, 1966, read: "I met with Sergeant T. on Hill 10 just east of Marble Mountain which then was the company position. He said he had patrol in twenty minutes and asked me if I was going to lead it. I said I would let him, would come along to get used to the terrain and the platoon. It was night as we left. When we stopped, the platoon set in a perimeter and dug in for the night. We moved out at daybreak and surrounded a hill located to the southwest of Hill 10. As the lead squad approached from the south, I heard automatic weapon fire. Without a word, the first squad moved up to a point just below the crest, covered from our own fire but on the hill. Then I heard an explosion, a scream, and the cry, "Corpsman, Corpsman!" There was no fire so we advanced to the top. There lay what I thought were two badly burned Marines, both legs gone, one man so badly burned that no one knew who it was. Methodically, Sergeant T. called in a helicopter, and the bodies were loaded aboard. Later I found out three Marines had been killed. This was my platoon. I hadn't ever commanded nor even met the dead Marines. We moved off the hill. I will remember the smell of burnt flesh and the sight of those men to my death. I had yet to see a VC. The platoon hadn't had time to return fire. I wondered if the automatic weapon was to draw us up on the hill." Another entry on March 1, 1966, went on: "Today we packed up and moved out to the air base. The previous day seemed unreal. Three Marines charging up a hill one minute and dead the next. It didn't seem as if life could go out of a body that fast. It is going to be a long thirteen months."

These words hit me hard. He hadn't been there three days, and he had seen his first action. In such a distorted world of dying, killing, and wounding, how could they go on day after day and maintain their sanity? I suffered with Jack in the insecurity, the first real test of his ability to depend on himself.

In April and May 1966, many large operations were conducted in South Vietnam. Although the news covered them ably, normal reporting could not describe detail of the individual actions. Operations such as Utah, Texas, Liberty, and countless names are all but forgotten except by the thousands of Marines who participated in early 1966. In May 1966, we received a long letter from Jack describing one of these operations, Georgia. Enclosed with the letter was a day-by-day diary. He said, "These were the roughest twelve days of my life."

The flat statements I later read did not or could not describe the horrible agony of war. I pray to God that time will eliminate or soften these memories. In his diary I read; "After several anxious days we left Da Nang by transport plane at 0800 on April 12 and arrived at An Hoa at 1100." An Hoa was a small airfield originally built by the French, located about 40 miles south of Da Nang at the base of the mountain separating Quang Nam and Qunag Tin provinces. The air strip and nearby Vietnamese compound made the area important. Also, the region was one of the few tracts in South Vietnam with a potential mining industry for copper and tin.

"We were put on alert immediately. Fifteen minutes later we were moved out by AMTRAC (amphibious tracker) to reinforce M Company and L Company who were in contact with an estimated battalion of Viet Cong. We hadn't been briefed very well. I didn't have a clear idea of how serious the situation was. We crossed the Son Ky River and disembarked from the tractors. When we landed, I gained control of Ky platoon on the beach and moved out on line. I saw a dead Vietnamese boy, bound and shot through the back."

Jack later told me that this Vietnamese had defected as a Viet Cong in order to lead M and L Companies into an ambush that he almost completed successfully. When the trick was discovered, the Vietnamese interpreter attached to the company killed the traitor before any further questions were asked.

"Corpsmen carried out two dead AM trackers (in ponchos) as we began to move out. There were pieces of flesh and bone in the sand from causalities on both sides. I still didn't know what had happened. There was no firing going on nor any signs of L and M Companies. Air strikes could be seen about one thousand meters north." The two companies had taken 14 killed and 68 wounded. About 18 Viet Cong had been killed, Jack later revealed:

"We waited all afternoon and then moved in the direction of L Co., replacing M Co. we returned to the An Hoa Base. We were directed to a new location in order to allow the withdrawal of M Co. As I was deploying my machine gun teams to a more covered position, I started to tell my machine gun leader to spread out his men. Suddenly a sixty mm mortar round landed about twenty-five meters from me in the middle of the team. I saw Corporal Morse running towards me yelling, 'I think Sgt. T is dead, and they got the lieutenant....' I assured him I was all right. I went over to where the first mortar round had landed. Cpl. Timmins, machine gun leader, was lying there. One leg was blown off at the thigh, the other at the calf. All that remained were stumps. He was screaming, 'Oh God, Oh my God. I know I am hurt bad. Oh God, the pain!' I ordered the doc (corpsman) to give him a double shot of morphine and yelled for the other corpsman. The wait seemed interminable. Cpl. B was next to Timmins when the round landed. Little could be done. B. had a jagged hole through his face, had lost much blood. He lay dying, and I knew it."

Jack's company was pulled out of the area after killing about four Viet Cong and silencing the mortar attack. How futile it must have seemed. Witnessing the ghastly deaths, coping with the heat, the men who went into shock, must have been in hell. He never speaks of it.

In October 1966, while visiting in New England, a freak accident occurred wherein I sustained a fractured neck. The doctor notified the Red Cross or someone. Three days later, I received a phone call from San Francisco. It was Jack. From a hill, known as the Rock Pile, he had been plucked literally by helicopter, given an emergency leave to see his mother. Bob had come from the west coast, Karen from home. I didn't know whether to be worried or flattered.

Jack spent much time at my bedside. Restless, nonetheless he felt obligated to stay in my hospital room. He was a tortured example of war nerves. I believe he talked more of the war than he planned, believing I was asleep. Very thin, he was nervous and jittery.

My heart ached for him and the thousands of other boys involved in this strange war. One night there was a celebration in the small town, a great display of fire works. Jack jumped uncontrollably each time a rocket or flare went off. It was no show to him, too much like the real thing.

I dreaded the goodbyes all over again. I hated to have him return to the DMZ. With my newly acquired knowledge of the battles and its people, I was more fearful than the first time. But relief at seeing Jack still intact was a great comfort to me. I am sure having him there speeded my recovery.

I know it was a great strain on him. Knowing of my accident forced him to travel half way around the world and back, made me feel guilty. I consoled myself with the thought that perhaps the trip had saved his life in some skirmish.

It was difficult for him to keep himself in check while home, feeling he should not upset me while I was defenseless, flat on my back. It must have been doubly hard for him to so suddenly be snatched from the throes of war and dropped into civilization in America where presumably life was continuing at a merry pace, with people oblivious to the deprivations, suffering, and horror existing in Asia. I'm sure it must have caused an inner revulsion, a bitterness.

Jack finished his Vietnam stint in March 1967. This time, he stayed on the west coast a few days, at his brother's, eating all he could get, sleeping till afternoon. I think he wanted to rid himself of some tension before facing Mom and Dad. I think he dreaded the readjustment to home, the meeting with former friends and their inevitable questions.

After a short leave, Jack again left the country to join up with a Marine Battalion already in the Mediterranean with the sixth fleet. I couldn't believe my ears when two weeks later, the brief war in the Middle East broke out. Are we to go through all this agony again? Is our son going to be forced into a war situation again?

As it turned out, the most discomfiting outcome for the Marines was a curtailment of shore leave. Because of the outbreak, many ports were not visited. The ship remained at sea on the alert. Three months later, Jack received the Bronze Star Award for his outstanding performance in Vietnam. In the lengthy citation, he was commended for his brave action in many operations, among them Georgia. The quotes from the newspaper clipping from Palermo, Sicily were as follows:

> The Bronze Star with Combat V was given for displaying professional skill and bold initiative while serving in Vietnam. The citation read:
> For meritorious service in connection with operations against the enemy in the Republic of Vietnam while serving in various capacities with the Ninth Marines, Third Division, from February 1966 until March 1967. During this period, First Lieutenant Kaye participated in seven major operations and numerous platoon and company size actions deep within enemy controlled territory. Throughout, First Lieutenant Kaye displayed exceptional professional skill and bold initiative. As a platoon Commander with Company A, First Lieutenant, Ninth Marines, from February 23 to 15 May 1966, he courageously led his platoon on Operation Georgia, a battalion-size search and clear mission in Quang Nam Province. His aggressiveness, sound judgment, and tactical knowledge inspired his men and contributed significantly to the success of the operation. While serving as a Platoon Commander with Company G, Second Battalion, Ninth Marines, from May 16 to 21 November 1966, First Lieutenant Kaye participated in five major operations, including Operation Hastings and Prairie. During periods of intense enemy action, he repeatedly exposed himself to hostile fire to effectively direct and control his platoon. Deploying his unit against North Vietnamese regular troops, First Lieutenant Kaye utilized his vast combat experience to efficiently direct the intelligence collection efforts of the Battalion. His skillful analysis of intelligence information was of vital importance in planning combat operations against the enemy. During the initial phases of Operation Chinook, First Lieutenant Kaye worked tirelessly and with great acumen in coordination of his efforts with staff and command elements, ensuring maximum support of the tactical situation. His exemplary performance and professionalism inspired all who serve with him and contributed significantly to the accomplishment of his unit's missions. First Lieutenant Kaye's exceptional professional skill, superior leadership, and unswerving devotion to duty throughout were in keeping with the highest traditions of the Marine Corps and of the United States Naval Service. For the President, V.H.Krulak Lt. Gen., U.S. Marine Corps Commanding.

Jack's first real contact with girls was when he started dancing school in fourth grade. He shuffled up to the nearest girl for a partner. By the third lesson, most of the boys had discovered girls were not all one size or shape. Some were easier to look at and easier to shove around the floor. Jack was not particular. If he had a choice, he preferred no girl. However, if the teacher became tough, he reached for the closest one.

As he grew up, Jack had a knack for choosing girls with problems, the more complex, the more interest. For the next ten years, each girl he went with found his vulnerable spot and played on his sympathy. Either she came from a broken home, her mother was in a sanitarium or she had a rare malady herself. It reminded me of the stray animals he used to attract. One girl, Judy, remained rather constant through college. If his stint in Vietnam had not become more important to him, she might still be around.

Pam, our youngest, was born when we had been married for nineteen years, a phenomenon which has made her more precious and miraculous. Closest to her in age was brother Jack whom she adored. With the nonchalance of youth, he tried to ignore her. Acknowledgement of her presence was to unobtrusively stick out a foot to trip her as she toddled by. In retribution, she had her own tricks. If Jack was looking at comic books, she would approach quietly from behind, snap off the light, then run out of reach giggling at her cleverness. This brought reaction. Even if she suffered a swat from him, it was worth it to see him so irritated. Try as I might, I could not impress Jack with the wisdom of ignoring her.

At age two and a half, she developed tantrums. No former experience had prepared me for this crisis. Doctor W. warned me to maintain control, not "let her get away with it." How so much noise could come from such a tiny girl, I'll never know. It was as if by the very shrillness of her screams, she could sway Mother. Painful as it was for me or anyone else within hearing, I sent her to her room, remaining pleasant but firm. It was will against will. I don't know what the modern method of dealing with tantrums is. I have seen mothers give in to avoid embarrassment.

Because she was the youngest in the family and the neighborhood, we had to find a way to get her with children. Consequently she started Sunday school at age two, nursery school at age three, delighted to discover there were other little people in the adult world. At four, we entered her in another nursery school at a girl's private school. At the end of one boring week, she had learned to suck her thumb! The teacher suggested kindergarten would be more to her liking.

After a conference, she entered kindergarten with the understanding she would repeat the year. At the end of the year, she passed the test for first grade.

Another conference resulted. To me, it was advisable to repeat the year as planned. Socially, she was young, physically much smaller.

Skilled and well coordinated, nevertheless she was careful. Much as she would like to be otherwise, she has never been able to ignore caution, to adopt a casual assured manner. We decided to have her repeat kindergarten. I think it was a wise decision. To be the youngest in the class can be a handicap.

Her childhood was uneventful. She was a delight to us, her parents. More outgoing than the others, she adjusted well to grown-ups or children. At age ten, she wanted to go to overnight camp for the summer. Remembering Karen's reluctance to go at all, we decided to provide the opportunity while Pam was so interested.

First day of school, camp or any form of regimentation is notoriously awful, especially when you are young. When Pam went to this northern camp, it was with a friend, therefore less painful. Also the novelty of an overnight train trip was distraction enough to obliterate most fears.

I was not along to witness any tears, disappointments, or discomforts if there were any. When we visited later in the summer, the sun was shining, and everyone was organized. We did not have to endure the many damp, soggy days of that summer.

One winter, we took a short Caribbean cruise. The single important factor that resulted from that fourteen-day trip was the acquisition of a houseguest for nine months. We met a friend in South America who displayed a desire to have his twelve-year-old daughter spend a year in the states. With great magnanimity, both John and I proffered an invitation for Sari to stay with us. Apparently from their point of view, the whole matter was settled then and there.

Before I realized it, we had a permanent houseguest in Sari for nine months of the following year. In theory, this is an excellent idea. In practice, I had my misgivings.

Sari was fat, placid, happy, and sweet. Schoolwork or any form of labor was of no concern to her. Raised in real luxury, she didn't know how to wash her own stockings. The head of the school more or less accepted her on my recommendation. By the time the Spanish department had translated any decoded reports from South America, it was obvious she was not a good student.

Sari arrived with no clothes suitable for winter weather. That first week was harrowing. Each day after school, we shopped for so many of the things a child needs for fall and winter—school uniforms, sweaters, books, jacket, raincoat, shoes, ski jacket, gloves, heavy socks, mittens, and rubbers.

If you set out to find opposites, you could never have done better than Pammy and Sari. Pammy was a doer. Sari was more interested in siestas. In fact, if she didn't understand her homework, which was most of the time, she closed the books and considered the matter final. We had envisioned learning to speak Spanish, but, as we should have known, the only one who learned a language was Sari. Her English improved rapidly, even became Americanized. All we learned was *buenos días* and *buenas noches*.

The two girls had separate bedrooms but shared a bath, which was the cause of many scenes. Pammy had lived with her own private bath. Sharing was all right with her as long as it fit in with her plans. Sari had never been to camp or had to share in any way.

Invariably they raced to the bath at the same time. In all fairness, Pammy was better at it and gave in to Sari, though not gracefully. Considering that Pammy was the hostess, this was correct. However, it didn't solve the problems at hand. If she didn't capitulate, Sari slammed to her room, wailing in a weird, chantey way. At first, I thought she was singing. Horrified, I discovered it was genuine caterwauling, either in anger or sorrow.

There were many such crises that kept life interesting but made a nervous wreck of me. Very often at breakfast time, Sari would announce she needed tennis shoes or some item unobtainable at eight in the morning. Her mother was in New York for three months, which presented complications.

Sari telephoned her nightly, which seemed to satisfy them both. I feared it would make her homesick. It didn't. The real flaw of the nightly Spanish reunion was the questioning of my authority. It was difficult to explain what I expected or what I thought she should do when the answer invariably was, "I'll call my mothairrr—"

I'm sure the child had dreadful moments, pushed into an American family she didn't even know. I talk too fast and mumble. That first week must have been a maze of bewilderment. Sari followed me around not knowing what to do. Pammy studied a lot, didn't want to be interrupted every other minute.

This was a development that stupidly I had not anticipated. I didn't know what to do with her time either. Sari always claimed she had completed her homework. I suggested she could improve her English by reading, starting with the simplest fairy tales. She liked the idea. Together we went to the attic, emerging with armfuls of children's books.

This endeavor accomplished its purpose, to keep Sari occupied and also help her comprehension of the English language. At the same time, it had its devastating effects. In no time, she advanced to the Caroline Drew books, the easy mysteries, and gobbled them up like quicksand. Soon, it became apparent that reading was the only thing she was going to accomplish. School work and all else was second in importance.

About this time the school discovered that Sari was not putting her all into homework—in fact, in mathematics, she was getting a straight E or failure. At the end of the first three weeks, she was put back a grade, which made an uncomfortable decision for the school.

Previously they had stated there was <u>absolutely no</u> place available in the seventh grade. With the language barrier and her chubby immaturity, it was a wise decision. At that, she tutored in math all the school year. Sari was intelligent, had attended a fine school in her native city. Perhaps the standards were not as strict.

After many despairing, frantic consultations, I said to the head of the lower school, "Let's pause. Sari is not worrying about anything. Her family is not worrying. She will be here only for a year, so the school shouldn't be worrying. Why don't we all relax?" It proved to be the best solution, ending a series of circuitous discussions.

Life settled lightly on Sari. Nothing affected her deeply. At times she forgot to write home, and we would receive frantic cables from Caracas. She never seemed enormously enthusiastic. On the other hand, she didn't appear unhappy. Pammy forced her to run around the house for exercise or to have a snowball fight, but the initiative never came from Sari.

Because she had never seen one, we took her to the circus. She was slightly impressed but mostly indifferent. Pam was infuriated. "She just doesn't appreciate all you do, Mommy." She would wail to me in private. It did seem so. But I would give myself a pep talk, reassuring myself that someday, perhaps years later, Sari would look back on this strip of living in the United States as a great experience, an integral part of her education.

We provided swimming lessons, riding lessons, although she was not athletically inclined. She ate enormous amounts of food and grew wide as well as tall. I tried to interest her in dieting. Smiling, she shrugged and kept on eating.

After the unsettling first weeks and months, the girls became fast friends. Although their temperaments, tastes, and way of life remained essentially poles apart, they had fun together. There was genuine sadness when it came time to part.

We had a vacation house in Michigan on a cold, sparkling lake. Sailing and water skiing were the main events. After two years of camp in Vermont for our youngest daughter, the novelty had paled, and Michigan and family looked tolerable.

Pam entered every race with her snipe. There were very tense moments that year. Most racers were a team, two brothers or brother and sister. Pam had no regular for crew. Each week, there was a crisis until crew, weather, and race had all been determined.

I flatly refused to get involved. I am absolutely rotten in competition. Also the thought of perhaps being personally responsible for Pam losing a race was too much. Not so her father who offered to crew. Watching from a distance, I shuddered at the apparent lack of understanding between captain and crew!

Captain Pam barked orders which John was either reluctant to follow or did not understand. The result was disastrous. I admired his courage at even attempting to sail under his own teenager. At the same time, I thought it foolish, an invitation to trouble.

Many times, I felt like ducking the whole issue. Whether I liked it or not, I got involved. Once Pam and Gwen, her crew for that day, were becalmed before the race. I had to tow them to the starting line. Hovering around the waiting sailboats made me extremely nervous, fearful that I would accidentally hit one. A tougher mother would just have left them becalmed. But the children could always successfully play on my sympathy.

Another time, they tipped over, the mast stuck in the mud. Trying to maneuver the speedboat around this perilous position without plowing in to them or the snipe was hard enough. To help right it and tow it, intact, was a chore. To me, the whole procedure had a nightmarish quality.

When the following summer, Pam wanted to return to camp life, I raised no protest. A sailing camp on Cape Cod was the choice. This time it proved more practical to drive her there. First day of camp was enough to make me want to take her straight back home. Eight girls to a cabin of questionable cleanliness was a challenge in housing to the assorted groups who landed there. Counselors or wiser "old campers" already occupied all the lower bunks.

While Pam was checking in with the nurse, Sister and I attempted to make the bed for her, an upper deck on an iron bunk. The mattress and pillow were mildewed and dingy. I think the pillow was filled with straw—at least it crackled. My imagination went to work.

Hoping to dispel disturbing thoughts, I quickly threw clean sheets over the dubious mattress and tried unsuccessfully to make square corners. The bed sagged so much, it was impossible to make it neat even if we could reach the far side, which we couldn't. Equipment, showers, and even the sailing boats looked ancient. The counselors were young, swelled with their own importance.

The former head of camp had died. Grandfather still survived, a typical old salt. Despite his advancing years, he showed more sense than the younger spryer leaders. Fortunately, we had signed up for one month only. This in itself should have warned me. Reliable camps do not condone halftime attendance.

As it turned out, the camp and its facilities were just as bad as I surmised. After four weeks, Pammy returned nervous, weepy, and ten pounds lighter. We did not realize that she was headed for a serious illness. Concerned over the weight loss, I took her to the doctor. Unfortunately, this particular doctor was disgusted with overweight pimply youngsters and told Pam her slimness was great.

Her physical development slowed, she became increasingly nervous, irritable, and temperamental. On advice of my obstetrician, we next visited a famous endocrinologist. Diagnosing the case incorrectly, he put her through many tests of pituitary gland x-rays. Suspecting a thyroid gland, he prescribed medicine for same, which only increased her tension.

In the midst of this, I was laid up for many weeks in an out-of-town hospital. Our woman of little work (she called herself a housekeeper) quit as soon as she learned of my accident. This left Pam to be bundled from house to house to stay while my husband tried to commute to see me. For most young teenagers, this would have been heaven. For Pam, it was disaster, the final touch that sent her health and weight catapulting to a dangerous low.

When I returned home, by ambulance, Pam continued to worsen. By December, disgusted with lack of progress, my husband changed doctors, took her to a local clinic of renown. More tests, consultations, and weeks later, a name was tagged to her illness. Name or not, this did not solve anything. Thin to the point of emaciation, her very life was endangered. She was hospitalized for seventeen weeks. The psychological gastro-intestinal reaction was coupled with many problems of emotional basis. That winter was a horror. Pam tutored in two subjects which kept her mind occupied somewhat.

Brilliant in her studies, at the end of the school year, she won the French prize, received an A in math, and passed all her exams—without attending a day of school the second semester. The following September, she went away to a ranch-type school in the west.

We drove her out. Opening day was bewildering. Parents were lugging bags, duffels, and suitcases. Most new students were gaping, too confused to be efficient. Six girls to a "suite," three in a room, and one closet. A bathroom containing a tin shower stall, lone washstand, and toilet looked unsatisfactory for all those females.

Mothers were resolutely unpacking, sorting, advising. No one looked particularly surprised. So I started stuffing drawers and hanging clothes. I stole a glance at my husband who looked amazed at the performance. Somehow I think boy's dormitories are more adequate.

After Pam's severe illness, it was not surprising that she was unsure, scared, and homesick. My husband and I were alone for the first time in many years. But not really alone. We made six trips to the west that year. Phone bills were astronomical. But we felt it important to give all the support we could. Somehow we all weathered that school year.

One dramatic incident was scary. After a trip to Mexico, Pam suddenly developed blood poisoning, perhaps from an old ski injury, perhaps from a Mexican insect. Instead of meeting us for a weekend of sun, swimming, and dining out, we raced to visit her at a city hospital where she was confined to bed with heavy doses of penicillin. In June she returned home, still thin, still on crutches, and begging to attend school locally and live at home. To this, we agreed, though reluctantly, with misgivings. Away at school, she had captured every scholastic prize, had made some good friends, and had grown more independent. To return to her former school and classmates appeared difficult to me.

The summer went well. She took an elective course at summer session, played golf, tennis, and was relatively happy. School began after Labor Day. With great enthusiasm, she entered all work, sports, and clubs.

By November, she lost her grip, stopped eating, and became thin and nervous. Eliminating all the events and doctor visits preceding her downfall, suffice it to say, she was hospitalized, forced to drop classes, and cease all activities. Her will to live was slight. How do these things happen? What did we do wrong?

Pammy has not yet found her niche in this world. I am confident she will. Her empathy, understanding, and intelligence have all been developed. Someday, perhaps we can treat it lightly. For now, we endure and pray. None of us knows what lies ahead for any of our children.

3

MARRIAGE

No matter what the age or the circumstances, it seems once a mother, always a mother. The trick is to know when to keep quiet. Most of my married life, I have felt like two people, my loyalty being strained constantly. Should I live wholly for the children? Wholly for my husband? Often I think a career woman has definite advantages. Children don't expect her to always be there. Just today, I heard a top woman executive comment on the subject. By the nature of her demanding business, she commutes, seeing her children only on weekends. "This way they really get the better part of me, my undivided attention."

A second benefit is that husbands cannot expect the same measure of perfection in household management if the wife is not solely a housewife. Even the word housewife denotes a drab existence. Doctors, tax men, repair men, all men in general still assume a housewife is home tending the house! Therefore her time is relatively unimportant. "She'll call again if she wants me." I wager a man's call is returned far more promptly.

On the freeways, I drive carefully but fast. I have noticed it infuriates a man to have me pass him. Even if he doesn't want to travel at such a rapid pace, he will invariably step on the accelerator until he has passed me and is again the leader. Usually this type slows down to his normal speed after he has maneuvered the lead.

But returning to specific examples, my husband still calls in the middle of the day. If he doesn't reach me immediately, his opening sentence, uttered with a degree of astonishment, "I tried to reach you. The line was busy!" My youngest daughter said accusingly, "Where were you?" I murmured weakly, "I answered on the third ring." "Well," she said, matter of fact, "Usually you answer on the second ring."

Undoubtedly it is my fault this condition exists. I should have started differently. The truth is, with my own family at least, I am delighted when they call. The only time I am seriously annoyed is if I am in the midst of a watercolor, which is at the exact stage to float in more color or accent. Somehow I cannot ignore the ringing phone.

My husband and I have had a good marriage despite bad years. At this point in life, I think it is healthier to dwell on the positive. Marriage is a full-time job. As a girl of twenty-two, I was ill-prepared for such a career. Married in the depression, we were fearless, thankful that my husband had a job. I was unused to scrimping or saving. Perhaps that is why I enjoyed it. I wouldn't trade those days for anything. Sharing our troubles, material and spiritual, gave life a deep meaning.

Many young people today have so much. Many have not experienced the joy of accomplishment after deprivation. In those thin years, I did a great deal of volunteer work, handing out bread loaves to the hungry, weighing babies at the clinics, helping underprivileged children at the fresh air camp. Each experience made me rich by comparison.

Our entertainment was meager. Entering every contest that was advertised, we worked diligently, hoping to win a prize. We never did. With the confidence of the young, we went off on a honeymoon to Bermuda with little thought to the future. John felt I should have the best. Our trip to the island was in an outside stateroom on A deck. Our trip back was on D deck below the water line.

Only on our return trip did he seriously face the fact that we had no home. Dividing our stay with both families, I spent endless hours looking at places to rent. One of my new sisters-in-law advocated an apartment in the neighborhood where she started. Dutifully I inspected those available in this territory. Buildings were old and the woodwork dark. I had never known apartment living. From the bedroom window, one had a view of the fire escape. Frosted glass made up the bathroom window what was directly opposite a similar situation in the next building. Such a cheerless home depressed me so much that I burst into tears.

Eventually we rented the top suite of a two-family home in a happier neighborhood. Because the landlord took a liking to me, he reduced the rent by five dollars a month if we refrained from any requests for refurbishing. To this we readily agreed. Doing the woodwork washing and kitchen painting ourselves, we converted it to a fresh abode.

One major disaster proved costly. I cleaned the living room walls with wallpaper cleaner. Flushed with my success, without pause I tackled the ceiling. From a ladder, I made sweeping swaths, carefully kneading and changing the cleaner often. I didn't take time to stand off and view my results until halfway through.

At this point, my neck and shoulders were aching with fatigue. I was slightly dizzy. Flopping onto our couch, I gazed at my efforts. Horrified, I realized the ceiling was streaked beyond repair. To be truthful, it had looked better dirty. My husband gulped when he saw it but was reasonably consoling. Of course we ended up having the ceiling repapered.

Our happiness was great. Pleasures were simple. My one extravagance was a laundress, a Hungarian woman who helped me so much. For three dollars a day, she washed and ironed the bed linen, the shirts, daily laundry, washed the kitchen and bathroom floors. If there was time, she did windows. I felt like a queen. Mother once told me, "Never learn to iron a shirt and maybe you will never have to." She never did!

Later when the children complained of our dull existence and our stodgy ways, I ruminated over those early years. On our first anniversary, we had a party. It was a tricky business buying the alcohol, distilled water, juniper drops, and making our own gin.

Disguised in a punch, it was not bad. We invited forty guests. About sixty came. The punch did its work. One guest fell down the front stairs, another down the back right through the screen door. Being young, no one was hurt. Everyone thought it was funny.

During prohibition, we went to many nightclubs or speakeasies. In my college days, I thought it was a status symbol to have cards from the correct places. I felt worldly ringing a bell, showing my card to gain admission to a densely smoked room serving alcoholic beverages. No one questioned age. All that mattered was keeping out the "Feds." Fear of a raid was the only worry.

In a nightclub, we took our own jug of homemade corn liquor, keeping it in seclusion under the safety of the tablecloth. Setups were ordered at outrageous prices. Cover charges helped make up any deficit to owner.

When repeal finally came about, no one knew how to act. Although the beer was 3.2 percent alcohol, such openness and freedom was a challenge. One felt obliged to have a drink whether wanted to or not. Home entertainment in those earlier years didn't faze me. The butcher taught me about meat. To him I took my problems. Eight for dinner. How many pounds? How do I cook it? How do I carve it? He never failed me, probably saved me much money.

People were content with little during the depression of the 1930s. Everyone's position was identical. If we entertained, bridge was the recreation after a buffet supper. A movie or a play was a rare treat. Each generation undoubtedly thinks of the trite phrase, "Give me the good old days."

Personally, I do not want to return to the small hardships of our earlier life—the bucket-a-day hot water heater that in reality required twenty buckets of coal to maintain water hot enough to do laundry, the clothes wringer you cranked by hand, and the absence of TV. But, at the same time, I do not envy the young married couples of today who start out on a grander scale. They are restless, nervous, and have little to work towards.

In earlier years, the task of earning a living had to come first. I resented it. The children did also. I found it particularly hard to adjust for many reasons. First, my Dad had been strictly a nine-to-five executive. Nothing changed this. Business did not trail him home. Undoubtedly more security of job and possessions make a difference. Whatever the reasons, I thought all husbands had to be the same. Second, I discovered a woman's feelings do not correspond with a man's. No matter how deep their love. I was thwarted constantly. I had been used to small luxuries, did not mind doing with less, but I thought love was the answer for anything. From my first home-cooked meal, I discovered marriage was not what I had imagined.

Remembering Dad's hours, I fixed lamb chops, peas, and mashed potatoes for six o'clock dinner. When John arrived home at eight, the chops had shrunk, the peas were a shriveled grey, and the potatoes were watery. I was shocked. Soon, I learned business came first.

My entire married life has been geared to the needs of the family, the hours they were required to keep, lunch boxes to pack, and the familiar morning rush, work, school, and appointments. We never lived near public transportation, a situation in which we involved ourselves by choice. This necessitated much chauffeuring.

Now that my husband has a little more leisure I find the mornings equally frustrating. Still we get up early, but there the similarity ends. After breakfast, he sits down to read the paper and make phone calls. This is fine until this slower pace involves me. For years, I have trained myself to get all difficult, unpleasant tasks done first. I think better in the morning. Also, I am not as flexible as in earlier years.

If my morning is organized mentally, I could weep with rage when my husband decides to sit and chat. More likely, he will ask me for a particular paper that should be neatly filed. Of course it usually turns out that that is the one paper that is NOT in place. As I frantically search my confused desk, my husband sits and waits patiently, smiling good-naturedly at the chaos I am causing.

For example, this morning I planned to leave the house at 9:30 (housework all done), swim at ten, hair appointment at 11, go to bank at 12:10, luncheon meeting at 12:30, doctor appointment at 2, shop for daughter's baby, stop at daughter's house, market, home again to prepare dinner. At 9:25 a.m. my husband wanted a list of bank figures.

"Can't it wait until tonight?" I wailed.

"This will only take a minute," he replied.

One thing led to another. John left at 10:15. I abandoned the swimming and felt resentful. I know I'm unreasonable but there it is.

Would I go through all this again? Would I encourage others to have a child in later life? What are the benefits? Let me hasten to say, emphatically, YES. I would go through this again were I to have a second chance.

Physically and psychologically I show the strain, particularly of the past three years. Spiritually and intellectually, I have grown. Which is most important? While I was pregnant with Pam, my trips to the dentist increased tremendously. Now my back bothers me. Maybe it could be traced to late pregnancy. On the other hand, with the exception of one great traumatic experience, I sailed through the menopause without any discomfort. I have noticed this is true of many older mothers.

My hair is whiter, the lines are deeper. But who can say this would not have been true anyway? At the same time, because I do have a critical teenager, perhaps I am more careful of my appearance, more conscious of the trend. My skirts are shorter. I am active physically. I make an honest effort to keep in a size eight or ten dress.

Emotionally, the strain has been shattering. During the first weeks of Pam's hospitalization, I ran the gamut of emotions—shame, guilt, insecurity, and remorse. I tried to analyze too much, see where I had failed. Slowly came the recognition of which we must always be aware, "Yesterday is gone. Tomorrow may never come." All we are concerned with is now.

To overcome these emotions, I had to draw on faith and love of God from whom I gathered strength. Forgotten words of power came to mind, the paradox. "When we are weak, then we are strong." (2Cor.12;7-10). "Our Lord does not give us a higher burden than we can carry."

I have often longed for peace, rest, and a calm life. If such came to pass, I'm sure I would be miserable. Just recently I have come to realize this is so.

4

TRIPS

When I was in the first grade, Mother, sister, and I went to Florida with Grandmother and Aunt Kate. It was a long trip from the Middle West in those days. We went by rail, changing trains in Washington. To a youngster, the ride felt interminable, the only diversion being the tour to the dining car at meal times. Sleep did not come easily at night. In the dark, it sounded like the wheels were going faster and faster, hurtling around bends in the roadbed at a terrifying speed.

Many times during the night, the train came to a grinding halt, each car bumping the one ahead, and then lurching on cautiously I would raise the window shade. Sometimes we were at a station. Other times we were in the middle of nowhere. I worried, convinced that something was radically wrong to cause a stop at no destination. Often a stifling smoke pervaded the car. Then I knew we were going through a tunnel.

When at last we reached the south, it was a delight to step out into warm sunshine. Mother was conservative, however, and did not approve of a quick transition from cold to hot and watched for any infraction of the rules of dress. Embarrassingly, we had to wait a day before shedding the long underwear; then another twenty-four hours before graduating to socks.

For this trip to Florida, we stayed at the Hotel Urmey in Miami before Miami Beach was developed. Grandmother was pleased to have the two daughters-in-law and grandchildren with her. In as much as it was her treat, she felt entitled to be the boss.

We went to a large municipal pool to learn to swim. It was a harrowing experience. The teacher was a brisk woman dressed in a tank suit with a lifesaving emblem on it. This in itself was pretty unorthodox. I had only seen swimming attire like Mother's, which consisted of a black satin-skirted swim dress with black tights (Annette Kellermans). Grandmother said no lady showed her bare legs!

At any rate, this questionable lady taught me to swim by having me enter the deep end. Then, in any fashion I could, I stayed afloat to try to catch the long bamboo rod which she held enticingly just out of my reach. When I got to the point where drowning appeared imminent, she would relent and tow me to the side of the pool. Mother fretted about the deep end because, with all her fancy bathing outfits, she couldn't swim. As I couldn't touch bottom at the shallow end either, it didn't make any difference. Psychologically, I guess it did with Mother.

This vacation was typical of resort areas of the day. With the American plan, emphasis was on good food. I woke very early; for the peace of all concerned, Mother let me go to the dining room alone. I was waiting at the entrance at seven for the doors to open. Usually I was the sole occupant. Guests were geared for a more leisurely pace. Ordering alone and signing the check made me feel very adult.

Mother was naïve in many ways. She signed up for a sailboat ride, which lasted several hours. We all suffered severe sunburn. For all her supervision in shedding winter clothes, she was uninformed on the power of the sun. None of us could swim, and I recall no life preservers either.

At that time, Miami Beach was a wilderness. There was a bus that took passengers across a long, rickety wooden bridge from Miami to the beach. I was a timid child, and this ride frightened me. Many planks were missing on the bridge. From the bus window, one could look directly into the water below. With boards clattering and thumping, the entire structure seemed too flimsy to withstand one more trip. Literally, I prayed all the way over and back. When the others asked why I was so quiet, I was ashamed to give them the reason. Once there, we changed to bathing suits in a smelly, wooden bathhouse. Then it was fun, romping and playing in the water only to our knees. However, each time I lived in dread of the travel to and fro.

The Hotel Urmey felt obliged to entertain their guests. Accordingly, once or twice a week, they put on a dull concert of chamber music. One time, we spent the interim racing up and down in elevators, playing hide and seek. The audience was sh-sh-ing, straining to see whose obstreperous children were so rudely interrupting the program.

Mother was torn between disdaining to recognize us or having to reprimand or punish us publicly. Finally, realizing that we were known anyway, she had to stand up, collar us, and send us to our rooms. I'm sure she was more mortified than we were.

Vacation was almost over when, simultaneously, sister Barby and I came down with the measles. Mother was more worried about the hotel finding out and evicting us than she was of our state of health. From another hotel, she sent the laconic message, "staying on in Florida." Understandably this infuriated Dad who assumed Mother was just recklessly extending her vacation. It required several telegrams back and forth to get matters straightened out.

With shades drawn, we remained in bed, whisking off our dark glasses whenever the maid came in. Whether or not this secrecy was successful, we continued our stay at Hotel Urmey, emerging two weeks later, pale and wan, but with no complications.

Many childhood vacations were taken minus Dad. I guess he preferred to take adult trips and couldn't take time to do both. Mother was nervous riding in an automobile driven by somebody else. Yet we traveled to Watkins Glen, Niagara Falls, and Cedar Point.

Restrooms were non-existent. Mother was not hesitant on that score. Marching up to a farmhouse with a child at each hand, she smiled ingratiatingly, inquiring, "May my girls use your outhouse, please?" Once Mother got so involved, we ended up having milk and biscuits with the farmer's wife.

These sojourns couldn't have been fun but, doggedly, Mother continued to make them, believing it was broadening our education. To be realistic, when you are young, there isn't any appreciable difference in the White Mountains or the Green Mountains.

Looking back, I remember small, unrelated incidents from these motorings. Watkins Glen reminds me there was a frightening fire that night. I worried about the smoke, the chance of survival. Of the beauty and splendor we went to see, I recall little. Likewise, the White Mountains trips bring to mind a car burning from over-used brakes. Mountains here are hazardous to cross. We stopped often to let the engine cool or rest. At such times, Myles, the driver, rolled huge boulders to brace the wheels, eliminating the danger of losing the car altogether. It was comforting to see the rocks firmly in place. Only then could I enjoy the relax-and-stretch period.

One summer, we took a vacation with both Mother and Dad. Dad drove. Detailed instructions on how to motor to various places were all contained in the Blue Book. Great concentration was required to follow it, though. For example it read: "Take right turn by red school house. At second white house, turn left onto cinder road. After crossing bridge, turn right up long hill, etc. etc."

We went to Groton, Connecticut, to a summer resort on the water, staying at a large rambling hotel with superb food and lots of white wicker furniture on the veranda. Meal times were of prime importance. As a guest, you paid for the three meals a day. Consequently, everyone ordered more than they could assimilate comfortably, wading through soup, fish, entrée, salad, and dessert even at lunch. Such gorging was agonizing.

One noon, a band played the Star Spangled Banner out on the terrace. No one paid the slightest attention. Annoyed at the lassitude of the diners, I jumped to my feet, stood saluting the flag during the entire rendition. Partly for shame at the lack of patriotism of the people, partly because I knew I was a forlornly conspicuous spectacle, I blushed furiously. It ruined my lunch. I was shocked at my own sister who I felt should have given me visible support in this. She was merely embarrassed for me.

During the day, we climbed the huge rocks on the beach, dug for clams, sat in the wet sand, letting the waves rush over us as the tide came in. There was dancing every night. Mother let us watch from outside. With the men in white flannels and blue coats, the women in billowing chiffon or lace, it looked gay. To see Mother and Daddy actually on a dance floor was a new experience.

Dad was not a good dancer, but Mother was very popular. Men loved to dance with her. Light on her feet, she was always laughing delightedly. I felt stirrings of jealousy or worry. Never had I considered Mother as being sought after by men. But even I, young and ignorant, recognized the smile and pat she gave to Mr. K. was far different from the tender, understanding looks that passed between Dad and her.

At a reasonable hour, Mother excused herself, personally tucking us in bed and cautioning us never to open the hotel bedroom door. Then she returned to her friends and dancing. We drifted to sleep to the refrain of the current popular tunes. Though our parents were not with us constantly, we were secure in the knowledge that we were loved and needed.

One of the less successful trips was to Canada, a plan that was conjured by Father. Dad found a little-known spot in Canada that catered to families, was sensibly priced and dull, even for children. As we drove up to the site, a family baseball game was in progress. I so hated baseball that the thought of having to participate in a game with strangers made me vomit right then and there. It was not an auspicious beginning.

We went with the Masons, which in itself was strange. Dr. Mason was our minister. Although he shed his collar and robe when informal, he still remained primarily a minister. It didn't seem proper to be on vacation with him.

Mother liked Mrs. Mason who was large and jolly with an infectious laugh. The Mason girl, about the same age as my sister, was a pastey-faced, sniffling creature with blackheads around her nose. Some allergy kept her pale eyes watery. Her personality was just as disagreeable. Bob, the boy in the family, was a brat.

One interesting thing about him was his eyes—one was blue, the other brown. It gave him a strange, eerie appearance.

In contrast to the plush resort in Connecticut, this Canadian one was like a family camp. A huge bell gonged out the meal hours where we ate at long tables. Mother liked good food and really suffered on this score. Menus were heavy, filling stews, boiled potatoes, and rice puddings. One sixteen-year-old girl, Dolly, became the idol and ideal of every teenager there. With golden, curly hair, she had the bluest eyes I had ever seen. Plump and dimpled, she wore outfits of baby blue and ruffles.

There was no planned activity for children or teenagers, but, admittedly, Dolly was the leader. Whatever Dolly decided to do, it was the in thing to do. Once it was sliding down haystacks, another time, an obstacle race. One evening, it was a contest to see who could eat the most mustard. I have never been able to tolerate mustard on anything since. Dolly thrived on admiration, and was just as delighted with the hero worship of the young as she was with her contemporaries.

Sister Barby went away to camp in Maine when she was twelve. It was not as well managed as advertised, and she had a miserable time. Forced to continue to ride horseback with blisters already raised on her bottom, these became infected. Food was poor. She came home thin and nervous. Listening to this experience did not heighten any weak resolution I might have had to go to camp. However, the next summer, Barby planned to go to a different camp near Ashville, North Carolina.

This time, the family investigated more carefully, checking references, consulting former campers. Suddenly I decided it would be a good test for me. Apparently I did not consider expense or the fact that it was a privilege to go.

During the long train ride to North Carolina, I had plenty of time to regret this decision. I was lonely, shy, and scared. Sister Barby was no help at all, located on a different hill in senior camp where I rarely saw her. I was in the junior section in a kiosk with five other girls and a lovesick counselor.

I'm sure Chunn's Cove was like hundreds of other camps before and since. Life was regimented, bugle call for rising, rush to cold showers which was mandatory, flag raising, breakfast, and then the schedule of activities. Camp was one major crisis after another as far as I was concerned.

First came the swimming test, a grueling thrashing the entire length of the icy, spring-fed lake. Next was the canoe exam. Paddling to the middle of the lake, you dumped, fully dressed. Then the trick was to shed clothing, including high-laced tennis shoes, right the canoe, bail, and return to shore. After surface diving to bring up a ten-pound rock, I thought I had overcome the main trials. But no—everyone was ordered to dive off the board headfirst. Each time I got to the end of the diving board, I chickened out, backing off. In time, this requirement too was conquered.

Riding was next in importance. I was afraid of horses and still am. For a while I felt relatively safe on a beast called Squirrel who was lumbering and gentle. During the second summer, I went on an overnight ride, which shattered any confidence I had acquired. I was assigned to a small, spirited mare, Country, who was tough, ornery, and kicked the other horses, so we were relegated to the end of the line. At this point a thunderstorm came up, and it was questionable who was more frightened, Country or I.

Overnight walking hikes were supposed to be a great treat. In retrospect, it may have been muscle building, but anyway you look at it, it was a lot of work. Sunburn was still a problem. To keep from blistering, I wore hat, gloves, long stockings, and long-sleeved shirt, all of which did not add to the comfort of the trip. Furthermore, I was small.

For some reason I could never understand, the bigger, sturdier girls led the line, striking out at a vigorous pace up the mountain trail. By the time the end of the line caught up to the resting spot, they were off again. It was a gasping struggle with shoulders aching from the pack. To omit one of the blankets from the poncho roll was a temptation. Air was icy in the mountains, so it was better to sweat in the daytime than shiver all night.

When we reached our destination after an all day hike, there was no time to relax. Our leader designated jobs. Often it was to the spring to fill the water pails, a third of the way down the mountain again. Wood had to be gathered for fires, and provisions unpacked from the truck, which followed us. If you thought about it, the entire performance was pretty silly. But, after a supper of canned beans, wieners, and Hershey bars, singing camp songs around the open fire brought about a warm camaraderie that cannot be duplicated. This, I guess, was the ultimate goal of all that work.

Of course, there were times when the starlit night didn't materialize. Then we shrank under our ponchos on the ground in a heavy rainstorm, feeling the water oozing underneath. There was no place to go for protection so we just rolled closer together for warmth and security.

The last week of camp was filled with nostalgia, tear-jerking performances, awards, and goodbyes. Train letters were written to best friends whose names were forgotten in the years that followed. I'm sure it built up some character, but when my eldest daughter balked at attending camp I didn't force her, remembering the first year I endured. Ever since those two summers, I've had a great respect for homesickness. An indescribable feeling like seasickness, there is little to do about it at the moment. You just have to live through the painful process.

Although I went to a few camp reunions, it was never the same again. Seeing girls and counselors dressed in city clothes, away from the habitat where we had shared so many personal experiences, they looked out of place. We found we were strangers, with nothing in common but memories. It was heart breaking. I preferred to skip the reunions and stay with the recollections that became rosier with time.

When I was sixteen, Mother planned a trip to Cape Cod at the Hotel Belmont. By this time, Mother had become a little more accomplished at driving, but sister and I were only fair at it. Not trusting our ability to decipher directions, Dad armed us with a map mounted on a cardboard plaque, with the way clearly defined from home to Cape Cod.

In addition to all our baggage, we had stacks of books and hotel information. I didn't own a train case, so carried all my makeup in an open cardboard shoebox. This was unwieldy to carry in to the hotel each night but was more important to me than clothes. I had become a perfume collector, fancied I needed a different fragrance for various moods. It was bad enough at home, but lugging the whole contraption while traveling was certainly impractical. Mother was indulgent though and didn't complain.

On the third or fourth day, we were rolling along the highway in our Buick, when sister suddenly remarked, "If we don't stop soon, we'll be in the ocean." Mother jammed on the brakes, grabbed the poster map and discovered we were almost to Provincetown, the tip of the Cape. Dad inadvertently had neglected to tell her to stop at the red line so that we continued to the water. Sister and I howled with laughter at our stupidity. Mother was as cross as I'd ever seen her.

Dragging us up at dawn, she had calculated our arrival at the swanky resort in early afternoon, in time to get unpacked and cleaned up for the dinner hour. She felt it was important to make a good first impression, no matter what the situation. Therefore, it was distressing to her to pull up under the stately portal of Hotel Belmont, just as everyone was gathering, fresh and charming in their dinner dress.

We looked hot, dirty, and bedraggled, which we were. Even our luggage was battered and mismatched. My shoebox of personal belongings didn't add to the dignity. Our clothes unpacked wrinkled and messy. Somehow they didn't look nearly as snappy as we had thought. Mother was disgruntled, yearned desperately for Dad, wondering to herself how she ever managed to get involved in this trip with two teen-aged daughters. Even the headwaiter, thinking we looked pretty disreputable, ushered us to a table behind a pillar, a sure sign of insignificance. Mother was too tired to argue.

That vacation was a great success for sister and me, boring for Mother. All the young people met on the beach each day with blankets, portable victrolas, and bottles of vinegar to speed up the tanning process. There were early morning swims with breakfast on the sand afterwards. In the evenings, there was dancing. I was in awe of the older girls who had an air of assurance. They ran to the water, racing through the breaking waves until they hit a level deep enough to dive and start swimming. This debonair entrance into the ocean always produced a young man who followed suit. Even as I grew older, I could never quite manage this spectacular performance with the same nonchalance.

At the Cape that summer, sister met the man she eventually married so she was in a dream world of her own too. Her man seemed old and staid to me, but she was ecstatically happy, so I decided he must be right for her.

My children don't seem to fall in and out of love as easily as I did. I started going to parties and school dances young, but did not have a romance until I was sixteen. I was invited to a college prom, out of state. It was thrilling enough to be invited over long-distance telephone, but when Mother enthusiastically endorsed the idea, the ecstasy was complete. My classmates were equally impressed.

There was much preparation for this weekend. Mother was excited too, because she was going to chaperone. To this day, I think the two new evening dresses she bought me were the prettiest I've ever owned.

One traumatic event almost ruined the fun. I had three planter's warts on my right foot. Thinking to alleviate the pain, Mother took me to a chiropodist who applied acid to eat out the warts. This made the condition twice as painful and necessitated pad and bandage on the bottom of the foot. My shoes were new, dyed to match the sashes on the dresses and presented a real problem when I started to get ready the first night of the prom. Without hesitation, Mother took the razor blade and slashed the new satin shoe, giving more room for my sore, swollen foot. I was astonished at her ruthlessness but, in a vague way, realized Mother was reliving her own youth, aware of the importance of this first college house party.

These were the days of stag lines at dances. I never had a better time, danced incessantly, although with the combination of warts and new shoes, my feet were throbbing. The most dramatic happening was that I fell in love with a dark-eyed southerner from Memphis, Tennessee. Our song was "My heart stood still." To this day, when I hear it, just briefly, I catch my breath and my heart does stand still.

His name was Jack. He was a rotten dancer, young and awkward, but, to me, he was wonderful. He followed me to Atlantic City where we roamed the boardwalk, hand in hand, bought "our record," and made solemn promises to one another. For the rest of the year, he wrote every day, letters that were personally delivered by special delivery messenger.

When I hesitatingly first told Mother I had fallen in love, she did not laugh, she didn't even blink. "Isn't that wonderful dear," she said. "I have never forgotten the first time I fell in love," she continued. It seemed preposterous to imagine Mother being in love like this. I had been so fearful she would make fun of me. It was a miracle to retain this magic and continue my private dream world with dignity.

By the time Jack came to visit us the following summer, much of this magic had worn off. To recapture the glamour and tenderness of the first encounter was difficult. Our correspondence gradually trailed off, and we never got together again. Countless times after that, I rushed home after a party, telling Mother, "This time I really am in love." She always smiled patiently, and made the appropriate responses, never questioning these emphatic statements.

The vacation with Grandmother in Florida occurred when I was still a teenager, revolved around an era, a way of living that has more or less vanished from the American scene. There was a definite time element for the south. January, February, and half of March were the proper months, the logical time to avoid the northern winters.

Grandmother's life varied little. After Grandfather's death, her travels were confined to Florida or Atlantic City. Rooms and train accommodations were reserved well in advance. Nothing was slipshod or frantic about the departure. Rosie packed, Grandmother secured her new money and placed it in the money belt she wore around her ample waist. Her jewels were cleaned, wrapped in tissue, and deposited in a chamois bag, which she kept in her enormous black pocket bag.

Arriving in Florida, we were met by limousine and taken to the Hotel Flamingo where she stayed after the Urmey was torn down. The Flamingo, on the Bay, was simple but elegant, covering much land. Beautiful walks and gardens led the way to the swimming pool and the docks where luxurious yachts were tied up.

Because Grandmother was a creature of habit, her movements were predictable. First, she ordered a bowl of pecan nuts, which we cracked and ate, picking out the sweet, meaty bits with a tiny pick. Next a basket of King oranges, though they tasted better then, warm from the sun and fresh from the groves.

When we went to our first meal, Grandmother was very particular about the location of the table. It was important to her. She felt entitled to a good viewing seat from where she could watch the other guests, perhaps converse with guests at neighboring tables. Location had to be on the aisle, in the prominent position in the room, away from the kitchen noise, and out of drafts. Only after this was accomplished, did she tip the waiter. He was polite, understanding that if he gave the proper attention to these details, he would be handsomely rewarded. No words on the subject were exchanged.

This sort of consideration is not much in evidence today. Tables were set with white damask cloths and bouquets of fresh flowers. Waitresses wore long-sleeved black uniforms with starched, white aprons. Each table had its own girl. American Plan again caused us to eat great quantities of food at all meals.

Mrs. Hawkins, a handsome woman with silver gray hair, was the official hostess who found dancing partners or a fourth for bridge. Without a husband, this job was her sole means of support. Promptly at four each day, I showed up for afternoon tea which she so graciously served in the lobby. Mrs. Hawkins was not as charmed to find me a regular participant at these tea parties. Unashamedly she was looking for eligible older gentlemen to relieve her of the burden of self-support.

Overlooking her obvious boredom with a young girl, I continued to come, just so I could study her lilting voice, her expressive hand motions, and the easy flow of chatter, which was part of her magnetic personality.

Early in my married life, I made a trip with a group of women to Sea Island in Georgia. Our days were peaceful, relaxing on the beach, getting up whenever we pleased. Suddenly, John joined us, and the spell was broken. I managed to induce him to the beach, but not to sit. We ran, we sand sailed, we explored the terrain, but no more hours of staring into ocean and space, the soul-building peace that does such wonders for me.

John thought up countless projects, even without swimming. In the morning the vultures beat us to the beach, feasting gluttonously on the dead sea life washed up in the night.

Remembering this hectic activity, I refused to join a group who were planning a cruise. "John would never relax, he has to be doing something," I explained. Helen responded, "I'm going to ask John Kaye right now!" She returned in a few minutes with the startling statement that John thought it was a terrific idea.

With many misgivings, I sent in our deposit, secured a sitter for Pammy, and waited the day of departure with trepidation. John never mentioned the trip. Digging into our meager savings, I sent in the rest of the payment, which firmly committed us. About this time a dock strike developed that I thought surely would dampen his spirits. "Just don't take many clothes" was John's brief comment. "We will probably even have to carry suitcases."

This was disconcerting to a woman. Cruise experience had been limited to the short ride to Bermuda on our honeymoon, but I knew one needed many changes and dressy attire for dances and the Captain's dinner.

Not until we landed in New York did John express enough interest to ask where we were going! We sailed from New York the next morning in bitterly cold weather. After we had passed the Statue of Liberty, we explored our new floating home. To my amazement, John immediately entered into the spirit and tried everything. Up at seven, he headed to the gym where he rode stationary bicycles, steamed, and had a rubdown, and arriving for breakfast fit and trim. Sally and I walked the decks in the early morn. Later I swam in the indoor pool.

John and I took dancing lessons. Also, we entered every contest put on, limbo, costume, talent, champagne waltz, and races. It was all in fun. At least we weren't idle. The deck chairs we had rented were rarely used.

At each port, we went sightseeing or shopped. In Jamaica, John and I went to Doctor's Cove to water ski in the cerulean waters. Not until much later did it occur to me that there was plenty of jagged coral under that gorgeous green blue sea. Fortunately, we didn't spill.

None was more surprised than I to see John enjoying the cruise. Perhaps it was the novelty. Personally I think it was because it just happened to him. He liked the unexpectedness. Before each port, I read diligently of the island where we were landing. As for John, he relaxed, took it as it came, blissful in his ignorance. At times, I get a longing to travel, just John and me. So much to see, with time and money so much a factor. My dream is to see each family member settled in his or her own niche, then just go. Will such a carefree day ever come?

Many times we work too diligently on accomplishing a good time. The most delicious moments of life just happen. Often the anticipation, the planning afterwards, is far better than the actual time itself. One such trip was our western tour, when we had been married eighteen years and had three children.

For years we had planned to take them camping, to see the West. When Bob was sixteen, I realized suddenly, if the children were to accompany us, it would have to be soon. When my husband John actually agreed to take five weeks from work to do it, my enthusiasm was unbounded. Even the children became mildly excited, especially about the camping part. Today, we speak fondly of that trip. With each telling it becomes more fun and glamorous.

I wouldn't trade it for anything, but, to be completely honest with you, there were some pretty ghastly moments of that summer. Jack was nine years old and ornery. He never glanced at the gorgeous scenery, keeping his nose buried in comic books. His eating habits were atrocious. Realizing this bothered everyone, and he became worse. In Hannibal, Missouri, it reached a climax with a tense battle of wills between him and his Dad. Neither side won but the rest of us were miserable.

Another gruesome night was the one in Yellowstone National Park. We thought we were farsighted in making reservations ahead, which turned out to be non-existent. Settling for a tiny room in a shack with stilts, there were two cots for the five of us and no bath. With sleeping bag and blankets, we made out, but not happily. About five in the morning I awoke to see the sunrise, but it was not exceptional either, children were tired, cross and unimpressed with the scenery, with the bears, and sulpher springs. We were glad to leave.

We spent two weeks in Aspen, Colorado, in a rented cottage with all modern conveniences. From there we took side trips in an open jeep, up the face of Ajax Mountain and down the other side. For variety we visited an old ghost town and a marble quarry, and we picnicked beside the Colorado River. Suddenly, the children felt they were being cheated on the open life. Leaving the coziness of our electric blankets, we packed up tent, stove, and sleeping bags and headed out in the trusty jeep. Camping out at Maroon Bells, we boasted of the lark when we returned home.

Years later, looking back on the trip objectively, it truly was the most uncomfortable. Weather was extremely cold, with the peaks still covered in snow. John pitched a tent for me. Surely the tent kept out some of the wind, but all of us were freezing cold. The biggest surprise was Karen, our dainty thirteen-year-old who turned out to be the best camper of all, washing dishes, cooking, and carrying firewood.

Bob was determined to fish and envisioned pans full of fresh mountain brook trout. Fully equipped with waders, rod and reel, he cast long and diligently in the icy bubbling stream. Usually, his stern self-discipline and his patient vigil paid off, but this time we settled for canned beans, I still think the fish were frozen. We encountered snow at Estes Park and at Pikes Peak that summer.

Our journey up Pikes Peak was educational. Halfway up, we stopped to shift and secure the load on top of the car. That's when we learned about vapor lock and putting cold, wet rags on the fuel pump to relieve the crisis. Mounting these unusual heights, I sternly cautioned the children to take it easy when we reached the top, altitude and all, a warning which Jack and Karen completely ignored. They raced to the lodge for water, whereupon they both fainted dead away.

John and Bob had disappeared, and I was left with two sagging youngsters. Apparently, it was a commonplace event, because the woman at the soda fountain wordlessly handed over some smelling salts. Once revived, they looked at me with something akin to respect, astounded that I had heard of the effects of altitude.

The gigantic splendor and the grandeur of the west is a humbling experience. Awesome in their beauty and strength are the wonders of nature. Man seems small and inconsequential in comparison. At the same time, the moon and stars appear closer. One feels a proximity to a power greater than oneself.

Somehow, things come into better focus, and the pettiness and the doubts are dwarfed out of existence. Not as exciting as an African safari or an exploration into a strange land, but still our western voyage was satisfying and illuminating to us.

As a family, I believe we were closer than at any other time of our life. As a married couple, I think John and I shared a feeling of accomplishment, a satisfaction in seeing the children emerge as individuals. For the most part we liked what we saw. As new sights to see, the Great Divide, the Rocky Mountains, the National Parks were undoubtedly more soul satisfying than a foreign tour. To realize you are a part of this great land of America is thrilling.

One other western trip that John and I took alone earlier was to the Island of Victoria, Vancouver, and to Banff and Lake Louise during World War II. At Lake Louise, we got off the train much to the dismay of the conductor who assured us there was no way to get up the mountain, and nothing to see or do if we did.

Leaving our suitcases at the railroad station, we set out to walk. After a half hour of trudging, two workmen offered to give us a lift in their truck, which we gratefully accepted. They dumped some lumber and us at the top and went on back, cautioning us to "Look out for the bull moose on the way down—it's the mating season." Both of us stood silently a minute, drinking in the lonely beauty that is printed indelibly in my mind.

Presently, I am an amateur painter. At one time, I studied music and piano seriously. As always, great displays of beauty as seen in color, voice, a waterfall, or a snow-capped peak overcome me with emotion. I cannot clap after a brilliant piano recital, feeling shattered from my dream world when it's over and the artist is thanked by tumultuous applause. To me, the noisy reward seems inadequate and inappropriate for the great contribution of joy and beauty. So it was with my

first view of Lake Louise, a small emerald jewel nestled down between huge gla-
ciers. As we stood there, the only two human beings within miles, a gigantic snow
slide came crashing down before our eyes, with a thundering roar.

If the hotel had not been boarded up for the duration of the war, there would
have been countless admirers. But, for us, alone, it was like a private performance
to more deeply impress us with Nature's power. It was such an unbelievably
exciting drama; I have never wished to return to see it inhabited.

For me another unique experience was a trip to Europe with our elder son.
Bob was living with a Portuguese family and studying at the University of Lisbon. One goal was to become more fluent in speaking Spanish and Portuguese
for his orals towards his Ph.D. Always the economical one, for his two years in
Spain and Portugal, he never asked us for a thing.

After his year in Lisbon, I received a letter one day, saying he was going to
travel a bit through Russia, Czechoslovakia, Finland, and Norway and why didn't
I fly over and join him? I sat down and answered immediately. "Would love to
come, when?"

To this day I do not know whether his invitation was an idle thought or a subtle, bona fide invitation. I suddenly discovered, by the return mail, that I was
more or less a chaperone because a girl, Marsha, might join us. Even this did not
daunt me. Because I had no time to try to secure visas for the Communist countries, I settled for a meeting place in Stockholm in September. Whatever
prompted the invitation, I decided to be flattered and not question the motives.

The trip was fun, and I am so grateful I went. Often these unexpected
moments are the ones to grab. We drove in a tiny Renault, three of us, with suitcases, a balalaika (Russian guitar) two knapsacks, and a loaf of bread, jam, zwie-
back, and sardines. It was crowded, and the back seat was uncomfortable—too
hot, as the heater seemed to work exclusively in the rear. Up front, the top leaked
a bit when it rained, and I loved every minute of it.

Before long, it was evident that Marsha and Bob were in love. I was astounded
because he had never even mentioned her name. In New York, boarding the ship,
they had met, both with skis over their shoulder, creating an immediate bond.
Three of us were companionable. Bob did a marvelous job of showing me the
countries. In Stockholm, I had reserved a lovely room and bath in one of the better hotels. The young people never considered advance reservations. To pay over
one dollar for room with breakfast was exorbitant and foolish, to Bob's way of
thinking.

About every fourth day, I insisted on a "nice" hotel, racing to the desk to sign
up the room before Bob could find out how much it was. If he persisted in know-

ing the tariff, I glibly lied about the price. In time, he relaxed on this score as he discovered it was rather nice to "borrow" my bath or shower when he was staying in a fifty-cent room. We had an unwritten law that if only two rooms were available, Bob and I would share. I felt it might better preserve the good relationship I was establishing with my probable daughter-in-law, to give her some privacy.

Bob had no patience with extravagance. Once we landed in a small town in France with very little cash between us. However, Bob absolutely refused to let me cash a traveler's check because the hotel's rate was too high. The principle of the thing appeared to assume gigantic proportions in his mind, so I finally agreed to wait. As a result we had to drive the next day without eating, a distressing state, as I love breakfast.

About mid-morning, although the rate of exchange was still not acceptable to Bob, Marsha and I overcame his objections, cashed a check, and darted for the nearest bakery. What heaven to munch the delicate pastries, with flaking crumbs and powdered sugar over all.

Marsha and Bob were mostly interested in museums and historical sights. I shared this interest but also was anxious to shop. Again this was a problem, for we hit the cities on the weekend when the stores were closed. Mondays and Tuesdays the museums closed, so we were traveling on the road. My husband is not a shopper either, so I was used to quick decisions.

When I had the chance, I bought, not waiting to compare prices or even study the merchandise. In most cases, the purchases were good: stainless steel in Denmark, sweaters in Munich, and stretch ski pants which were still fantastically expensive in the United States. True, the pants were intended for my husband, but instead fit our youngest son. However, he wore them all through his four years at Dartmouth, so it was still a smart buy.

Bob and Marsha were clever with maps, always perfectly orientated. Circumstances permitting, I would wander out on my own, but first Bob would coach me in directions. Arming me with a city map, he put a fat X showing the exact spot I was on at the moment. East and west, right and left still remained a mystery to me. Usually, I thanked him prodigiously, letting him think I was in control of the situation. Striking out boldly, I walked out of sight, and then asked directions from a sympathetic listener.

Once, in Spain, my watch stopped without my knowledge. I slept soundly until I awakened naturally. I felt refreshed, sent for breakfast. A beautiful October day greeted me as I walked to the dressmaker's. No comment on the hour I arrived. Not until I noticed the locked grilled gates on the storefronts did I realize this was siesta time. In the distance a clock chimed two in the afternoon instead of ten in the morning.

A unique and enchanting interval, I was delighted. Not so Marsha and Bob. Suddenly I remembered I was to meet them at one and literally ran all the way back to the hotel. My breathless explanation that the "watch stopped" sounded pretty thin even to me.

Ever since that delicious lapse, I have made a point of leaving off the wrist-watch when on a vacation. We are so bound to watching time, that often when I wake up in the dead of night, I can accurately guess the correct hour before I check.

On the other hand, I suppose, we should be grateful for the awareness that allows us the choice of arranging the moments of the day. My mother was a victim of many strokes, bedridden for two of the four years she was ill. Her time was her own, but what could she do with it? She couldn't get up, couldn't even scratch her nose, so it made little difference whether she slept in the morning or night.

When Dad was agonizing through his last days of Carcinoma, he was under heavy medication to make the pain endurable. One day, he clutched me, panicked, "Eddie, I have lost one whole day in my life. I thought this was Tuesday. I see it's Wednesday, and I remember nothing about yesterday." My emphatic assurances that it really didn't matter were no solace to him.

To Dad, this lapse meant a threat of sanity. So, in these cases, losing time is not pleasant. But for most of us, in normal living conditions, the clock is a specter, hovering over our shoulder, warning us to ever be alert, spoiling our fun like Cinderella's.

I don't particularly envy the young parents of today, but in some ways modern innovations have made their life easier. One way is the mode of transportation. I well remember taking the two older children, aged three and six, to Florida, three days and two nights on the train. I did some pre-worrying about appeasing the energy of six-year-old Bob, but it was Karen who caused all the trouble. Refusing to eat, she spent the dinner hour stacking everyone's silver in her water glass. She balked at entering the washroom while the train was moving. Furthermore she kept us awake all night. At the end of the trip, John drove to Florida, and we returned home by car. Surprisingly, Karen was an absolute angel and slept all the way.

Years later, remembering only the charming naps, I ventured another trip south, driving fifteen-year-old Karen and eleven-year-old Jack Jr. This time we had our youngest, Pammy, who was then two and a half. She was a good baby. Naively I anticipated no trouble.

In packing luggage in the car, we left a sizable nest for Pammy, for naps and play in the back of the station wagon. Somehow John always avoided many of these jaunts of mine which just shows how much smarter he is. On this particular journey, we got an early start. Pammy refused to nap, but I was not alarmed, anticipating a more restful night. Sensibly, we stopped at five in the afternoon to have dinner and get to bed early. The doctor had suggested a little Phenobarbital, which we administered to Pammy. The rest of the way was a nightmare!

At midnight, Karen urged us to get up and start driving and (quote) "Leave before we get thrown out!" Pammy was still awake, fascinated with the three of us who were trying to sleep. She turned on the lights, methodically opened and slammed the glass shower door repeatedly. If this did not get the proper reaction, she had learned to manipulate the lock and raced up and down the corridor.

On the radio earlier I had heard a foreboding weather report, so the thought of heading further south didn't sound as foolish as it should have. However, I hadn't foreseen the dense fog that enshrouded the mountains of Virginia. It was a harrowing drive, following the narrow, twisting, and guardless road. The children were enchanted with the excitement.

Pammy's behavior was abominable. Still wide-awake at four in the morning, I concluded she must be ill. In Roanoke, I stopped at a hospital to have her checked. It seemed incredible that she could stay awake so long. They prescribed more Phenobarbitals, even though I had related our experience and her peculiar reaction. On the road again, the new dosage acted as a stimulant. It was unbelievable.

By nine in the morning, Karen and Jack whole-heartedly had entered into the spirit of adventure and said, "Keep driving Mommy." By that time I was exhausted, mentally and physically. Time to exert my dubious authority, I reasoned. Trying to find a motel room early in the morning wasn't easy. They don't want you at that time of day! Paying an outrageous price for one room, we managed to catch a little sleep. Pammy didn't settle down until noon.

In the afternoon we started driving again. On this peculiar schedule, we arrived in Daytona or Ellinor Village at an inopportune time the third day. Everyone had a good time except Mother and Pammy. In the circular they had advertised all the ease and fun of a carefree vacation. What it didn't tell you was how to cope with an uncooperative two-year-old. The nursery school turned out to be nothing but a place to check your child. Pam was wretched. The older children inspected it and after the second day said, "Forget it!"

Bob, who by this time was in college, arrived with several classmates. Each day he threatened to leave for Fort Lauderdale and the action. I urged him to go, by all means. Truth of the matter was, he was having fun fun fun right there, with free room and board too. Several boys stopped off to see Karen. One of her best girl friends arrived for a week's stay too. Jack tagged along with whatever group would take him, for I was completely grounded with Pammy. She developed a sun allergy, hated the beach, and longed for home and her own crib. The whole thing was a dreadful mistake from beginning to end.

Often the sights you travel the farthest to see are the least impressive. When I was small, Mother made one of her many U.S. educational tours, this time to see Niagara Falls. It was a tedious trip but the excitement of the forthcoming sight kept us going. Finally we arrived there to see the tumultuous falls, the thundering water spilling over. Wallace, ten-year-old son of Mother's friend, condescended to get out of the car, looked briefly at the celebrated falls, and then said, "Well, now where?" The effrontery, the letdown, rendered even Mother speechless.

So it was with seeing Japan at cherry blossom time, many years later. Here I was, a grown woman, disillusioned to find the majority of the blossoms were fake. Just as Yellowstone Park had been a disappointment earlier. I have been more impressed by a misty pink sunset in my own backyard.

5

JAPAN

Our trip to Japan materialized quickly. Sister Helen had fallen in love with Asia on two previous trips and now wanted us to see Japan before it became completely westernized. Secondly, Paul Rusch, leader of KEEP (Kyosato Educational Experimental Project) urged us to come. My husband is a director of KEEP and had not seen the project in person. So, if one needs an explanation for a trip, we had two valid ones. Without consultation, we simultaneously declared we would not make the trip without Pammy, our youngest. Too old to go half fare, but still young enough to tolerate parents, she was enchanted with the plan.

Sharing our feeling that this would be educational, the school she attended was surprisingly reasonable. So it was April 16th when we arrived in San Francisco for the first part of our trip. Pammy was charmed with the city and the few remaining trolley cars. The sidewalks were overrun with the new fad of skate boarding. Descending the steep inclines on foot proved unusually harrowing with youngsters whizzing by, perilously balanced on their wheeled boards.

First, we visited the Ong family who had arranged our trip. They invited us to their home, which contained many priceless Ming treasures, combined with the practicality of an American kitchen. Tya, Elora, Mark, and Lance, their children, attended public schools by day. In the evening, they went to classes in the Chinese school, learning the language, writing, and history of their country. This left little leisure for children or parents, but knowledge was of prime importance to the Ongs.

About noon of the following day, we boarded our plane. We had chosen Japan Airways, believing it would get us into the proper spirit of the country. The stewardess, dressed in kimono, served Japanese food with chopsticks. Strong headwinds delayed our arrival in Honolulu where we paused about an hour for refueling and checking.

Everywhere was the scent of exotic flowers. Dress was informal with the muumuus and gold sandals predominant. Honolulu was two hours behind the west coast and five hours behind our mid-west home. Already we were experiencing the fatigue of time changes and travel.

From Honolulu to Tokyo was another nine hours of flying. Pammy slept a great deal for which I was thankful. Sister Helen luxuriated in first class, paying several hundred dollars more to be able to stretch her legs. Another time, I'm quite sure I would forego the atmosphere and fly the Northwest route, which is shorter and uses faster planes.

We crossed the International Date Line, and somehow it was nine-thirty on Sunday night. By our watches it should have been about three in the morning. Easter Sunday just had been bypassed. Many snacks were offered aboard. They were served attractively, but the seaweed and raw fish did not appeal on that endless flight.

It was a tremendous relief to land in Tokyo. First impressions of this largest city in the world were millions of lights. Beautifully colored and intricate signs, much more impressive than Times Square, lit up the city. A fast modern train raced overhead. Many road signs in English reflected the influence of the Olympic Games.

Paul Rusch and his assistant Rho were at the Okura Hotel to greet us on our arrival. Diplomatically they faded away promptly, knowing how weary we were. In the morning, they appeared again, bearing gifts this time. For each female, there was a silver bracelet with charms, typical of Japan with a fish, a teapot, a stone lantern, a pagoda, and a Toril gate. Other visitors waited for us: the travel agent, our future guide, the hotel manager, four Japanese businessmen, and a young couple, the Bakers from our hometown in the Untied States. The latter had been in Japan for four years, working for the Embassy.

After a confusing morning, we lunched with Bill and Peggy Baker at Zukuro Restaurant. Fish and rice seemed the safest choice. It was one of many unsatisfactory experiences for me. Eating with chopsticks was a difficult feat, but we disdained to ask for forks. Young three-year-old Charles Baker ate heartily of raw fish bits and gooey rice, three bowls of it. He was a solemn little fellow, pale, but healthy and strong. His Japanese nursemaid was anxious to learn English, but Charles resolutely stuck to his own code of speaking English to Americans and Japanese to the natives of Japan. Nothing would persuade him to change.

I had written to Peggy from home to see if it was possible to visit a Japanese school. I felt it would be of great interest to Pam and her own classmates as well. Peggy had arranged with a friend, Keiko Omoto, who took us to her alma mater, Atomi High School. Approximately two thousand students were enrolled in this girl's private school, which had been in existence for ninety years. Buildings and classrooms were similar to ours. Every girl wore a dark blue uniform and white headband. One unique factor stood out. Every head, without exception, was topped with thick, black straight hair that made even the head seem part of the uniform.

Giggling profusely, the girls constantly bowed when they passed us in the hall. Keiko answered our many questions about the school, particularly about the seventh grade. We learned they had ten subjects, Japanese, English, Mathematics, Science, Social Studies, Gym, History, Calligraphy, Art, and Music. Periods last fifty minutes with ten-minute breaks between classes. A typical school day runs from eight in the morning until two-thirty in the afternoon.

Before our tour, the director of the school served strawberry shortcake and tea. English was taught to the children, but the principal could not or did not communicate verbally. We managed to convey our appreciation with smiles and much bowing. In an English class the girls sang "London Bridge is Falling Down" and the "ABC" song, tittering bashfully between songs. A requirement was the calligraphy class, painting Japanese characters. This art is difficult, requiring long practice. Holding the brush upright, the figures are formed with a black ink, called Sumi. (Mo is the term used for Chinese ink.) It is in the form of an ink stick, made from soot gathered from burning the oil of plants or pinewood. It is then mixed with glue, resin, and perfume and molded into a flat or round stick. Western ink is a fluid. The ink stick is made ready for use by pouring a small amount of water on the slab or ink stone, called Suzuri, then rubbing the stick in the water. The degree of darkness depends on how long you grind the ink on the stone.

Pammy was already in love with Japan. The happy schoolgirls appealed to her. She noted the shortness of stature. Even the doorways were smaller than ours. I have no way of knowing the academic standings of the school. Certainly the children seemed relaxed and not as pressured as our Americans.

Again we dined with the Bakers at a restaurant of their choice, the Sukiyaki. Nobody volunteered information so the best plan was to stay alert and follow suit. At every home, restaurant or temple, shoes were removed and sandals donned. There was an abundant supply of foot coverings at the doorways. An exception to this was at the temples. I soon learned to carry a thick pair of warm socks in my pocket to shield my feet from the icy, damp floors.

The Sukiyaki was our initiation to a personally served Japanese meal. Shuffling self-consciously in our sandals, we were ushered to a room with a table a few inches from the floor. Pillows were in place on the Tantani or grass rug. I was grateful for the cushions. Perhaps it was in deference to western guests like us.

Dinner was cooked at the table on an individual stove, and then Japanese girls in kimonos, who hovered, anticipating every need, served it graciously. It is easy to see why most men like the East. Women wait on them and give them constant attention. I noticed on arriving at a hotel, my husband was not permitted to handle even his briefcase. He never got used to the idea of women carrying suitcases, which resulted in a slight embarrassing tussle at the entrance in a vain effort to uphold his dignity. However, the women were strong. Also they became insulted if they were not allowed to serve, so he had to give in with a helpless shrug.

Japanese beef is excellent. However, there were many times when I yearned for a steak instead of the usual boiled variety. Asians have adopted much of western life, certainly the ease of modern conveniences in many instances. But they scorn our food and ways of cooking it. If alone in a large city hotel, it is easy to get a good western meal if desired. On the other hand, if you are with a native, it is more polite to try to accept their ceremonial ways.

Since one of the reasons for going to Japan was to visit KEEP, we set out early one Tuesday morning, to catch a train to Kofu. It was pleasant to sit and view the countryside, ablaze with blossoms. I had been so bitterly disappointed in the cities at cherry-blossom time, to discover the majority of bloom was artificial, tied on to trees and bushes to impress the visitors. To stoop to using paper flowers seemed downright dishonest if not sacrilegious. But here, in the country, were live pink and lavender petals everywhere, vivid against their background of lush, dark green. Houses looked small and poor, but all had TV antennas. On the train, everyone had their own canteen of hot tea. It took us four hours to arrive at our destination, high in the snowcapped Japanese Alps. Mornings were bitterly cold. I recalled a friend's advice at home, "It will be very warm there in the spring." I was thankful I had disregarded this and brought my winter suit. Never once did I feel toasty warm while in Japan!

We toured the base at KEEP, whose mission is to provide food, health, faith, and hope for youth. The hospital was crude and dirty, but it meant a lot to the people in the area. Many had died needlessly before the medical aid KEEP had provided. My husband had interested our home church sufficiently to raise money for an ambulance. There it stood, a lovely shiny white Cedric car (Japanese make) with a bright, red cross on it. We felt proud to have been a small part of its inception.

Tramping around the countryside gave me a chance to see what the terrain is really like. Paul told us more about the country's resources. Much of Japan is mountainous, and there are forests. Japanese use their trees not only for lumber, but for charcoal to heat homes. Many trees are evergreens, but they also have bamboo, oak, and maples. The cryptomeria are plentiful.

Japanese are famous for Bonsai, or potted plants, which are dwarfed trees, trained to show the beauty of large normal trees. Most of the time, they use pines for this treatment. Each year, exhibitors may display their Bonsai or Bonkei at art shows. Bon kei (or Bonkei) are tray landscapes representing natural scenery only in miniature—stone, sand, plantings, and artificial flowers are used.

Recently, at one exhibition, there were two pines (Bonsai) reportedly each over five hundred years old. It takes loving, exacting care to produce the dwarfed trees. Main roots (about five inches in height) are cut away, leaving the small roots to develop. This is done periodically. Branches are curved by weights, or tied to form them into artistic shapes. They are kept in the shade and watched carefully. At least six to ten years are required to produce an artistic tree.

Perhaps you have not heard of KEEP and its work. Paul Rusch, a native of Louisville, Kentucky, went to Japan in 1925 to help rebuild YMCA units destroyed in the Japanese earthquake of 1923. He expected to stay about a year but became involved at St. Paul's University in Tokyo. There he taught English and Economics, before being interned the day of the Pearl Harbor attack, sixteen years later. During his stay at the university, he helped found the Brotherhood of St. Andrew in Japan and established the summer youth camp at Kyosato. More than seven hundred of his students claim Paul as their godfather.

Returning to the East in September 1943, he served under General Mac-Arthur until 1949 when he resigned and decided to devote all his time to KEEP.

The first years after the war, were desperate ones for Japan. Cities were gone, money, jobs, homes were non-existent. Between the years of 1945-1949, times were confusing, ripe for Communism to get started. Paul Rusch, working with a small group of young Japanese Christians in Tokyo, began studying the problems of the people. Rural areas contained sixty percent of the nation's people.

Paul and his followers felt the Japanese must learn to help themselves. Kyosato, one hundred miles from Tokyo, was the site chosen for the experiment. Paul had formerly constructed a youth camp there before the war. He and his group now acquired about nine hundred acres of land, high up in the Alps. The land was judged worthless for agriculture. Nonetheless, this group planned to raise food, bring health, faith, and democracy to the young people. Some of Japan's poorest people lived in this district, a hundred years behind the pace of the rest of the country.

Because the band of people was a Christian one, the first step was to build a church, a place to meet. Then evolved rustic cabins for schoolrooms and medical clinics. The food program was difficult, requiring three years to clear, plant, and actually produce some edible plants. By 1953, interested spectators were helping. A tractor arrived from Waterloo, Tennessee. In the next year, eight Jersey heifers and ten Herefords from Texas made the start of a cattle herd.

Kyosato church grew quickly and became self-supporting, with all members tithing. The main lodge of Seisen Ryo burned to the ground in 1955, which looked like an impossible tragedy to overcome. This building had been the center of all their work since 1938. Paul believed it was a miracle when friends from all over the world sent funds. Within a short period, enough money had come in to ensure rebuilding. Construction started in 1956, and the building was dedicated in July 1957.

Distances are far in this area. Travel is very difficult. Outreach stations were developed where local committees were responsible for their operation. KEEP's specialists and doctors went into the villages.

In 1956, again fire threatened to play havoc with the lives of these courageous men and women. Part of the hospital burned. Despite this tremendous handicap, that year 10,491 inpatients were cared for. Also 560 home calls took place. Thirty-six operations were performed.

In rebuilding the hospital this time it was constructed of concrete, making it practically fireproof. The government of Japan declared it a model for rural Japan. It is gratifying to see the healthy people, working the ground, learning, living, and loving together. Most of all, they love Paul, a really dedicated man who made so much of this come true.

Once, in Cleveland, Paul stayed at our home. A small, bald-headed man, he smoked cigarettes nervously right down to the stub. His health appeared shaky, and I worried about him for some time. Obviously, he was driving himself beyond endurance, realizing that our time in this earth is but a fleeting moment.

In October 1967 the dedication of five major buildings of KEEP's model highland farm school took place. Shortly after this, Paul celebrated his seventieth birthday, receiving cards and letters from all over the world. Towards Christmas, it was evident that Paul was failing, and he went to Saint Luke's International Hospital in Tokyo for a checkup. The electro-cardiographs showed a blockage in the heart.

After consultation and overseas conference, the doctors decided to fly him to Chicago to determine the advisability of inserting a "pacemaker." Dr. Igarachi, heart specialist, and Paul's adoring friend, Ryo Natori accompanied him.

The two-hour operation, placing the pacemaker in his breast, really saved his life. Through all this, Paul's one thought was always KEEP. A personal letter to us ended with the words, "Please pray and pull for me. I pray I can finish KEEP in time."

All those who see and know KEEP are heartened to see concrete evidence of success though one man's untiring effort to make a dream materialize. We inspected buildings, the muddy, smelly dairy, the pigsty, and the nursery school. Apparently the people are conditioned from early childhood to survive the wet cold. Every child in the school had a cough and runny nose. Windows were wide open but, as there was no heat in the classroom anyway, the outside air was probably better than the dampness of the building.

The rosy cheeks, which I had always thought were part of the charm of the cherubic children, were scarlet because their skin was chapped raw. Most of the three-, four-, and five-year olds had to walk several miles to get to school each day.

For lunch, some brought cold bits of fish or dried fruit from home. Hot rice was meted out at the school. As I see it, the trick is to survive those first tender years. If they do, the resulting adult is tough, strong, and immune to cold as evidenced by lack of overcoats or outer garments.

At Kyosato, there is a small church, simple, barren but proof that KEEP is built around the Christian faith. There are no pews, no heat, of course. Cushions of mats are laid on the floor on which to kneel.

The weather was cold, snowy, and the trees were ice-coated in the mornings. This was late April, and I wondered if it ever warmed up. We were unable to see Fuji at any time while at KEEP. The snow and clouds hid the majestic mountain. I had been unaware until I arrived there how elusive this famous sight is. I discovered many visitors are denied this view because of inclement weather.

We did get a momentary glimpse of another mountain called Kyosato. A Japanese friend, Koniko (Konni) related to Pam the legend of these mountains. The story was that there was an argument between the two mountains over which was the bigger, the masculine Mt. Kyosato or the female Mt. Fuji. A guide laid a pipe stretching across the two and then poured water in it that ran towards Mt. Fuji. This meant Mt. Kyosato was taller. Mt. Fuji was so infuriated that she picked up the pipe and pounded the head of Kyosato, breaking it into eight pieces.

Konni spent much time teaching Pam some Japanese words and characters. At a Pachinko Parlor, she gambled in an immense room completely filled with Pachinko machines. In front of each was a player, feeding it clinking silver balls, much like a slot machine in a gambling room at Las Vegas.

In retrospect, it appears we spent much time on the road, either on trains or cars. From KEEP, we returned to Tokyo where I had a brief time to shop. The department stores were modern with escalators and western merchandise. I wanted to buy Pam a kimono with obi sash. This turned out to be difficult. At a drugstore, an unlikely place, I found handsome purses for about eighty cents apiece. In the arcade of the famous old Hotel Imperial, we saw magnificent wall-paper for sale. I should have bought some.

The taxi drivers could understand no English at all. I kept a matchbox with hotel name and pictures of it. At least I knew I could get to home base if nowhere else.

From Tokyo we took a plane to Osaka, going directly to the Takarazuka Park where the world famous Grand Theater presented The Takarazuka Revue. Esquire girls paraded in gorgeous costumes, reminiscent of the Ziegfield Follies.

The Zukettes were a dance line, much like the Rockettes at Radio City in New York City. Girls are all from wealthy families, receiving only one hundred dollars for their work. Considered an honor to be selected for this group, naturally there are hundreds of applications. The show, which lasted all afternoon, was presented on an enormous stage. Costumes were elaborate. After intermission, a French musical comedy, sung in Japanese, was presented.

By this time we had acquired our guide, Hirohiko Tanaka (we called him Hiro), who traveled with us. Paying for his room and board as well as his guidance was a costly way to travel. However, in many of the places we visited, no English was spoken, and it is impossible to read the Japanese signs. Hiro was a small, polite man with definite preconceived ideas of Americans. I had the distinct impression that earning his living this way was most distasteful to him.

Apparently devoid of feeling, he spoke of his mother in flat tones. Once when I was admiring a colorful silken bag, I enquired if his mother would like one as a gift. This suggestion he squashed, adding that at her age, she went nowhere and could wear only black. Intrigued, I asked her age to which he replied, "She is very very old, fifty-one next birthday." Retiring in confusion, I decided to ask no more questions. The only semblance of emotion he displayed at all was at the shrines, where he always paused to pray—Buddhist fashion.

Many of the trains we rode were modern and fast. One of the most charming customs I found in Japan was the practice of playing tunes at each stop. I presumed each tune meant something. At least it was a warning that a stop was imminent. How much more acceptable and palatable than the mumbling, hog-calling type of thing we used to have in the United States.

As we watched the scenery from the train window, we noticed many flying banners shaped like fish. Hiro explained that it represented the carp, which is a strong healthy fish. Festival days are important and easy to remember for they date by number instead of month. For example, 3/3 is Girl's Day, 5/5 is Boy's Day, 7/7 the Star Festival and 9/9 the Chrysanthemum Festival. Legends, tradition, festivals, history, and heritage are vital to the Asian.

John had been feeling wretched with a virus. Adding to his discomfort was the damp, cold air we encountered everywhere. A dry, hacking cough kept him from relaxing. Sister Helen had been raving about the Issaen Inn which we were approaching, regaling us with stories of its being the Emperor's favorite spot; he must have visited it in better days. When we arrived there, I was horrified to find it looking rundown, dirty, and completely in Japanese style too, right down to the rock-like pillow with no mattress here and no heat either. I thought John was going to collapse. We put up a protest about the rooms, which were really firetraps, up steep, narrow stairs.

All of this caused great consternation with Hiro translating I know not what. When they showed us a western room, we embarrassingly had to refuse it, as it was far worse. There was a sagging three-quarter bed with a dirty, purple coverlet over it, no sheets of course, and much too short for the average American. Back to our attic hovel we went. I persuaded John to rest (on the floor) while Pam, Sister Helen, and I went to the communal bath.

I was very unsure of this procedure, but Helen was confident, anticipating her bath with great gusto. Personally I was extremely disappointed and thought the Japanese bath a product of the Dark Ages. At the Issaen Inn, they allowed five in a bath at one time. Fortunately or unfortunately we seemed to be the only occupants of the inns. At least it made the bathing a bit more private.

To do a Japanese bath, you sit on a wooden stool, low to the floor, and wash yourself thoroughly. Then you rinse by throwing buckets of water over you, removing all soap before immersing in a large, deep tub of hot water. As far as I could determine, this final bath water was seldom, if ever changed, thus the importance of the bucket brigade before entering. I couldn't help but wonder how many bodies had dunked in this tub before us. I was glad John had not joined us. He is so fastidious, I'm sure he would have been disgusted. We then dressed in ugly kimonos, provided by the hotel, and went to dinner, in a private room, served by little bowing Japanese maidens.

Food was supposedly western, in deference to our presence, some kind of beef. However, Hiro stuck to his menu of raw fish. We huddled together on the hard floor. I worried through the night, wondering if John would even survive that relentless damp cold. I could find only one toilet at this inn. It was slightly barbaric, being only a hole in the floor. However, with the lack of other guests, it was more or less private. Occasionally, I passed a figure scuttling in the dark hall, but never encountered traffic at the toilet.

The next day, it was raining in earnest, but we resolutely kept plodding on, glad to be out of the Emperor's inn. Sister Helen later told us even she had been disconcerted. After we retired, she rang for a masseuse. When the knock came, it was a man. She decided it was no time in life to get prudish, but I think her confidence in the inn was sorely tried.

We took a ferry across to Miyajima Island, which means Island of Shrines. It is a sacred island. No cremations, births or burials are allowed. As we approached the island, there was a huge Torri gate rising out of the sea, which at high tide appears to be afloat. In olden days, boats passed under it to purify the souls of the sailors. Many shrines dated back to the sixth century, which was the origin of Shintoism. We often tend to forget how young our country is until we visit some of the ancient ones.

At a shrine in the park are two large dog statues, one saying the first letter of the alphabet, the other the last signifying all knowledge begins and ends within the place of worship. There were booths to buy your fortune. If it is bad, you may tie it to a tree or bush and leave your troubles behind. Near the entrance of this famous shrine, which has not changed since the twelfth century, is a sacred horse, a live horse that bows continually as you approach. Nearby is a trough of water with a dipper. People rinse their mouths there to further purify themselves. Certainly the communal dipper did not seem pure but, you see, we westerners think so differently.

Hundreds of visitors arrive constantly to pray at the famous shrine. We saw a Shinto maiden in costume performing some kind of ceremony. Japan is in the Asiatic Monsoon Zone, so all natives are used to the weather. Everyone has a colorful umbrella. (Kase is made of split bamboo for the rib and oiled paper, with a waterproofed frame). School children have yellow covers for their book bag, which they wear, strapped to their back.

Our visit to Hiroshima made a deep impression on all of us. Pam became quite wrought up by the havoc the atom bomb had done. Sister Helen shared this feeling. Finally, I took Pam aside, cautioning her to reserve judgment until she had seen and studied Pearl Harbor on the theory that two wrongs don't make a right.

Historic bombing of Hiroshima occurred in the center of the city. What remains of the town hall has been preserved as an atomic memorial. A flame of peace burns under a large arch. In prominence is a stone coffin containing all the names of the victims. A sign reads, "Rest here in peace. Never again will we repeat our errors."

At the Hiroshima Memorial Museum, there were many horrible pictures, actual relics too, showing the effects of intensity of the heat. There were beer bottles bent and twisted but with beer still intact within. At one point, I became separated from our group. When I looked around the crowds, I was the only American present. Momentarily, I was frightened. At no time did I feel the Japanese truly like us. Perhaps this is a purely personal view, but at that moment, at Hiroshima, I did not feel safe. At the same time, a feeling of guilt or shame swept over me for our part in the destruction.

We took another train to Kurashiki, a small crowded city. Looking at the grubby, primitive town, I feared another Japanese inn. Imagine my delight when we entered the Hotel Kurashiki Kobusai and found it to be clean, modern, and equipped with contemporary conveniences. We had an eight-course dinner in the dining room. Reveling in the comfort of a real bed, we retired early.

Kurashiki is a town famous for its cultural center. Ottaro, a wealthy native, donated his collection of art works to found a museum there. Hanging are French paintings, perhaps only one of each artist. Included are some of the most famous by Renoir, Monet, Simon, Gauguin, Degas, Cezanne, Toulouse Lautrec, and Picasso. Also exhibited are paintings of Signac whose pinks, blues, and lavenders are brushed on in squares, giving it an appearance of tiny tiles.

There was a ceramics museum including the works of Shoj Hamada, Bernard Leach, and Kajiro Kawai. In the folklore museum, which was once an old granary, most of the work is pottery done by farmers. I was interested in a sample of a farmer's raincoat that was used in olden days. It was like a cape, made of rush, laced and woven to keep out the weather.

Between Kurashiki and Okayama is the best place to get rush for the Tatami mats which are on every floor in Japanese houses. The grasses grow four or five feet tall and are harvested in the fall. All Tatami mats are made in standard sizes, three feet by six. They last ten years with careful use. Again we boarded a train, this time for Osaka where a car met us and drove us to Kyoto, to the Miyuko Hotel.

Eagerly I looked forward to our five-day stay at the Miyako Motel, as John had been feeling miserable. Japanese living had not proved to be the delight I had anticipated. Our proposed accommodations at the Miyuko sounded comfortably plush with a chance to spread out. So much togetherness is a strain on nerves. To my dismay, when we were escorted to our quarters, it turned out to be a minute triple room for the three of us. John was too sick to argue, so I decided it was time to be firm. With the help of Hiro, I politely refused the room. Everyone concerned was just as polite, but also firm. I am not the aggressive type. However, I was genuinely worried about John's bad throat, wanting him to be comfortable. When the assistants realized I was being difficult, they summoned the manager who bowed and smiled ingratiatingly. After several rejections, they unearthed a lovely corner room with a bath, and an adjoining single room with bath. I almost hugged the manager. Pammy was equally delighted. Immediately she retired to her own bath, scrubbed, and washed her hair, reveling in the luxury of privacy. I understand the Japanese live in confined quarters with many occupants to a house. Rarely does one have a room to oneself. Bathing, of course, is family style.

I shooed John to a hot bath, I had just ordered up a hot toddy with the thought of keeping him in bed for at least twelve hours, when the phone rang. It was a charming voice, announcing that his friend (and I guessed, boss) was awaiting appearance and meeting with John in the lobby. Horrified, I stalled until John emerged, warm, and relaxed from his bath. Reluctantly, I told him a Mr. Sawai was downstairs. He groaned, but finally convinced me it was a business matter of importance. He promised to return quickly.

Again the phone rang. John's strained hoarse voiced croaked, "I know you are anxious to meet Mr. Sawai and Mr. Takumari. We'll expect you down in the lobby immediately." Then he hung up. Angered, I dressed quickly and went down to the big lobby. There sat John, looking white and sick, with two Japanese men, bowing and grinning. The president of the Japanese firm could speak no English, but his assistant acted as interpreter.

An insistent dinner invitation was the first gesture. I thought rapidly and came up with a reasonably plausible explanation of our inability to accept. The least variance from the truth makes me feel abominably guilty. I felt worse when Mr. Takumari whisked out a velvet jewel case, presenting it to me. I know nothing about pearls, but realized these were valuable.

Instinctively, I knew I must accept them as graciously as possible. This relieved their anxiety. Next, they produced a Kyoto doll for Pammy. By the reverent way they handled it, I knew this, too, was a unique and costly gift. I almost weakened on accepting dinner. After eyeing John, I decided I had better stick to my story. After a proper visiting time, we excused ourselves, returning to our rooms, laden with presents. We were safe for the moment, but knew we must continue this newly formed friendship by a reciprocal invitation.

The Japanese are proud of the former capital, Kyoto, its ancient history and culture. In the bombing of Japan during World War II, some feel Kyoto was deliberately spared because of its irreplaceable beauty and treasures. It has been said of Japan, "Tokyo is her brain; Kyoto her soul."

It would take years to see all of the temples and shrines. Some of the most famous types of art, architecture, and landscape are in this area, such as the strange rock gardens of Ryoanji Temple. This consists of white sand and fifteen rocks. People come from all over to view it, pause to meditate on Zen philosophy or religion. Personally, I could not drum up any enthusiasm or soul touching thought over this display. Some say the rake marks of the sand represent waves on water. I don't know what the rocks indicate, but they did not stir me one whit. Perhaps one must be a student of Zen to appreciate this.

The Golden Pavilion, originally built in the fourteenth century as a mansion of a shogun, or general, is now a Buddhist temple. Its graceful form, covered in gold leaf, reflects on a mirror-like lake. Because it looks exactly as you think an oriental temple should, it is satisfying to contemplate. Atop the upswept, layered roof sits a golden Phoenix bird, symbolizing the Messenger of Peace.

We visited a silk factory one morning when it was raining so hard it was not feasible to go sightseeing. Each time I wanted to shop, someone advised, "Wait until you get to Hong Kong." I should have known better, at least on the materials, printed chiffons, and flowered silks. All were unlike any I've ever seen. Sister Helen said later that she heard the dye was not fast. This fact did little to console me. I did buy scarves and bags, which I gave away too quickly. They were beautiful. A two dollar large scarf looked like a fifty dollar hand-screened one.

When John recovered sufficiently to brace the cold again, we planned a boat trip to shoot the rapids of the Hozu River that runs west of Kyoto. The clear stream runs in swift current through a deep narrow valley of rugged precipices and huge rocks. At the starting point, others joined us. It was quite a wait because the boats were still under repair. I wondered if they had to be put together after each trip. Soon we were told to get in.

The hand-hewn boats were large and awkward with a capacity of ten passengers, and each manned by a crew of four, two to row, plus one to pole in the bow, and one to take care of the rudder. Looking up at the high cliffs, we saw the colorful azaleas flowering amidst the rocks. It was a gorgeous sight. But with the swirling frothy white water ahead, I felt I must concentrate on some backseat driving. The man in the bow poled and pushed furiously to get us under way. Weather-wise, the usual cold, misty dampness continued, but the men who were responsible for our safety on the Hozu River were sweating copiously with the exertion. They wore white, cotton bands around their heads to absorb the perspiration.

At each turn, boulders loomed up ahead. When it threatened certain death or a smash up, the boatmen deftly warded off, only nudging the rocks. I'm certain the heavy sculls would have battered and broken up under amateur guidance. As the speed of the ride increased with the current, there was much gesturing and shouting between crew of the two boats that were riding the rapids. Later, Pam regretted it hadn't been more dangerous. I felt it was ample exhilaration for one day.

Because we had evaded the dinner invitation the first night, it did not free us from our obligation to Mr. Sawai. John was vastly improved with rest, a heated hotel room, and a couple of steak dinners. When a luncheon invitation came, we accepted. Mr. Sawai and Mr. Kataama called for us at the hotel and took us to Judanyai, a popular restaurant. We were ushered into a private room where we squatted around a large table low to the floor.

It is hard to know which way to sit. I wore full skirts and flat shoes as often as possible because it was easier to be more graceful. I tried sitting back on my feet from a kneeling position, tried sitting smack on the floor with legs to the side, and also attempted sitting cross-legged with knees out. This is where the full skirt was important.

The luncheon was a lengthy one with many courses. Anchovies came first, and then smoked salmon, seaweed, eggplant dipped into raw egg and the inevitable green tea. Chabba Chabba was the main course. A table cooker was in the center of the table. Into a pot of boiling water, the servers dropped all sorts of crisp, fresh vegetables, celery, onions, and leeks. After a reasonable length of boiling time, we picked up strips of raw beef and dropped them into the vegetable broth, then quickly in raw egg before popping them into our mouths. I tried desperately to cook mine rare but was so clumsy with the chopsticks, I never rescued the beef soon enough. It was frustrating and caused much merriment with the hosts.

Following the main course came vegetables such as cabbage and mushrooms. Then came rice with pickled things—-onions, radishes, ginger, and figs. Everything in this course was spicy and hot to the tongue. I also learned it was important to take a second helping. By this time my stomach was protesting. Surreptitiously, I slipped some Bisodal tablets to Pammy too, who was unsuccessfully trying to muffle burps.

Next came huge fresh strawberries, a welcome relief from the varied menu. More green tea was served. Then toothpicks were passed. By this time, it was four o'clock in the afternoon. We thought it would be impolite to excuse ourselves. During the entire day, Mr. Sawai was delightedly snapping pictures, sometimes of the food, sometimes of our awkward attacks on the food. I wondered later if the camera was even loaded. Perhaps film development is cheap in Japan.

One evening we went to a Geisha (Gay-sha) girl show, the Myako Odori, which means "cherry dance." It is held for one month at cherry-blossom time, starting about April first. Participants are girls who comprise the dance troupe, about a dozen singers who play the samisen, and ten others who play other instruments.

Before the performance, ceremonial Geisha girls, beautifully costumed, serve tea in the lobby. Rice-powdered faces remain immobile and expressionless. This isn't unusual since the Japanese apparently are trained to conceal their emotions anyway. The porcelain-like mask of the powdered skin must not be cracked by a single smile or frown.

Starting on her career early, from age ten to sixteen, the Geisha girl is trained in singing, dancing, music, etiquette, deportment, tea ceremony, and flower arrangement. When the gentle, womanly ways are thoroughly learned, the Geisha may be engaged for a period of from five to ten years. Her earnings go to her mistress to whom she is always in debt for her training and finery. She is a legend as a tonic for a tired businessman.

I, a woman traveler, was fascinated but disenchanted. In accepting the tea and cakes at the tea ceremony before the performance, I was uncomfortably aware of imperfections of the Geisha hostess. Although the graceful, fluttering hands were lovely to watch and the face was faultless, the back of her neck was not powdered. It was yellow and sweating undaintily. I guess I was too close. John flatly refused the tea which was thick, powdered green, and very bitter. Foolishly I was too polite to dump it, and the taste stayed with me all evening.

Ancient dances were executed by Maiko (apprentices). The Geisha, exquisitely costumed in colorful kimonos with brocaded obis, rendered music. They sang in a whining nasal manner, playing tom-tom like drums and samisens, a three-stringed guitar. With the advances and modernizations, there are not many Geisha schools left. I am glad we were there to see this unusual entertainment.

On the last day of April, we visited Katsura Imperial Palace, which required a special written permit. Pam was not allowed because she was too young, so the guide took her to the nearby Moss Temple. At the Katsura Imperial Palace, the gardens and buildings used about eleven acres. A bamboo fence enclosed the grounds. Scattered throughout are palm trees from Kyushi Island, over three hundred years old and many fine examples of bonsai. Prominent was a tea house and garden temple. Another work of art was the family-style Buddhist temple. Over three thousand stepping-stones and bridges are in the gardens, conjured up by the landscape architect Kobri Yenshu popularly called Enshu. At the main house, which is supposed to be architecturally perfect, there is a veranda for viewing the moon, especially at the time of the September fifteenth moon ceremony.

Great Japanese artists, architects, and landscapers use nature's background as part of the scene. A good example of this is at Entsuji Temple, which is noted for its gardens. As you gaze at the view of the Gardens, you see Mt. Hai in the distance as part of the backdrop, with tall pines in front of that, and rocks (Zen) and a courtyard of moss in the foreground. This is called the borrowing system, using nature's own background as part of the total picture.

Mr. Sawai and party accompanied us on this trip. I never saw anyone so busy with a camera. John is excellent and conscientious about keeping a record of travels, but Mr. Sawai was beyond description. I began to doubt the presence of film in the camera. Later he sent us some black and white prints, so I guess my suspicions were unfounded.

At the end of the tour, timidly we invited the others for luncheon. Hiro, our guide, had stated emphatically, "Japanese not go to American Hotel." But, with a little persuasion, they did. The Messrs Sawai, Katayama, Takashashi, and Hiro all resolutely turned their back on the western diet, but managed to order something sufficiently Japanese to please their palates.

Goodbyes were prolonged, with much more thanking, bowing, and agreeable smiling. Once Helen went to Asia, nursing an annoying back problem. By the time she returned home, the result of many weeks of bowing and bending had restored her to normal.

We had time for one more appointment that I was anxious to keep. Mr. Tokuriki, artist and teacher, gave us a demonstration of black and white brushwork at his home studio. He sat cross-legged on the floor. Holding the brush upright, he painted in an easy fluid manner. Rice paper, which is thin, grabs the paint quickly so the artist must know exactly where each stroke is to be laid.

Contrary to executing a watercolor on heavy paper, no pleasant accidents are likely to occur on this absorbent surface. Mr. Tokuriki graciously asked me to try it. Self-consciously, I made a few hesitant strokes that looked like nothing at all compared to his graceful birds and reeds. We bought a wood block and some sketches. Hiro, who had arranged the meeting, seemed pleased that we were interested in his native art.

On a wonderfully mild day, we left Kyoto on the Kiuki Nippon RR for Yamatoyai. We had six minutes exactly to change trains and transfer baggage onto the train to Matsuzaka. Each time we had these changes, I silently cussed the necessity of suitcases. Porters were either scarce or non-existent. Somehow we always made it.

At the famous Restaurant Wadekin, we ate Sukiyaki, cooked at the table, served with rice and tea. Wadekin-bred cows are carefully raised and are fed beer, which aids their digestion, supposedly producing better beef. Also they go through an exercise and massage program that distributes the fat, resulting in the most famous beef in Japan.

We went to Ise, headquarters of Shinto Shrines, to visit the Grand Shrine. Geku is the main shrine with architecture preserved for 2000 years. The followers of Shintoism pray at the doorway, clapping hands. The right hand represents the universe and the left hand, self. Clapping both together combines the two.

We traveled by car to Futamigaura Beach where the big attraction is two huge, black rocks; the larger is the male and the smaller, the female. I did not understand the significance, but many Japanese were sightseeing there. From there we went to Mikimoto Pearl Island. The late Kokichi Mikimote invented the method of cultivating pearls of hemispherical shape, and eventually he succeeded in cultivating round pearls. There is a museum showing the process of pearl cultivation from beginning to end.

The women divers, called Ana, wear white scarves around their heads, masks, white shirts, and white wrapped skirts. They used to dive naked from the waist up. This proved to be too much of a distraction for the foreign visitors. Toughened to the extremely cold water, some girls can stay immersed for a full minute, gathering pearl oysters to put in the round wooden tubs they wear around their waist.

Pearls are classified, not only for perfection, but also for color as follows: pink are the best, next silver, third blue and gold, and the dark pearls are from sick oysters. We left the island by ferry and then proceeded on to Hotel Shimakano at Kashikojima, a lovely view of Ise National Park and pearl islands.

We went by train to Nagoya, third largest city in Japan. Here we changed and took the new Tokaid Express train for Odawara. Traveling at a speed of 125 miles per hour, this modern train had a bar and lunch counter, buffet style. Reaching our destination, we went by car to Miyamoshita and Fujiya Hotel that houses guests and celebrities from all over the world. We had planned a cable-car trip the next day to see Mt. Fuji, but we woke to a wild storm where the rain fell literally in sheets. You could see great streams of it traveling across the sky amidst the fog and clouds. I was realizing more and more the possibility of leaving Japan without once getting a glimpse of Fuji. Being fogged in was a restful change of pace. We all caught up on sleep, letter writing, hotel shopping, and just plain contemplation of the many different customs and thoughts of the Asian world.

Many of their ways are in direct opposition to ours. It is said when a Japanese says yes, he means no. For instance, we might say, "We're not going to the shrine are we?" With the answer "No" (we are not). Japanese however, say "Yes" (we are not going to the shrine." It causes some little confusion.

Here are some other examples of opposite ways; Japanese books begin at the back—a letter is written in perpendicular lines top to bottom and is read from right to left. Japanese say east north rather than northeast and four or three, not three or four. Boats are hauled on the beach stern first. The man always precedes the woman and is served first at meals. When closed, the Japanese umbrella is carried handle down by the loop at the top. A man of Japan never praises his family, considering it bad manners to speak in a boastful way; he belittles his possessions: miserable house, good-for-nothing son, and stupid wife. Countless other mannerisms differ greatly from the west.

My overall impression of Japan was that though the people are polite, bowing, and grinning, they are, at the same time, pushing you out of the way. In no way are they subservient. Their toothy smiles reveal lots of gold and silver dental work. The country is literally teeming with people, short, stocky, black haired, and almond-eyed. They look prosperous and fit.

Every Japanese man carries a camera and is constantly snapping pictures. In the large cities, most wear western dress. At the same time, they retain much of their own Japanese culture. Their love of beauty, color, and flower is evident everywhere, even in the street where huge bowls of potted flowers are on every corner.

Early one morning, we boarded the M.S. Kohku Mara to cross the Inland Sea to Beppu. It is reputedly one of the truly beautiful scenic trips. Unfortunately, the morning hours were completely fog-bound. The steamer had to proceed cautiously, dodging the islands. There are three thousand of them formed from mountaintops of land that sank into the sea.

Japanese school children crowded the ship. This congestion is found at any spot you visit. The people believe strongly in showing youngsters their own country. We usually encountered great herds of raven-haired children, dressed in their navy blue uniforms. Many times we were the only Americans, and we were the sight to behold—more of a phenomenon than the spa or waterfall that teachers had brought them to see.

Our Pam was under constant observation to which she was completely oblivious for a time. But when the boys started ogling and poking her to see if she was real, she was aflame with self-consciousness. Cameras clicked, children giggled, and little ones grabbed their mamas and pointed at us.

By noon, on the boat ride, the weather suddenly cleared, and the scenery was magnificent. The snail-like pace of the morning made for a late arrival at Beppu, which was regrettable because the Suginoi Hotel was one of the nicest on our itinerary. We didn't have a chance to enjoy its luxury.

Pam slept in the sitting room on the floor, Japanese style but with an actual mattress, very comfortably. On arriving at the hotel room, the first courtesy extended is tea service. No matter if it is noon or midnight, a girl brings a tray of green tea and handless cups, a charming gesture. Nevertheless, to my taste, the tea has a strange flavor and a sickish green color.

The next morning, we took a train (The Sea Gull) to Miyaguma-guchi. It went in a tunnel underwater to get from one island, Kyosato, to Honshu. The train is an important mode of transportation in Japan, and the stations are always densely crowded. Train stops in Japan are extremely brief. If you were disembarking, you really had to be prepared to leap and throw baggage. Hiro was of tremendous help in these cases as he could alert us in advance.

Sundays appeared to be wedding days. At each stop we often saw bride and groom boarding the train garlanded with flowers. Usually the whole family was present with cameras clicking furiously. Dressed in western style, straw hat, and suit, the bride sported new luggage (which she carried herself). The older women of the wedding party were often in traditional kimono and headdress. No one wore coats.

As the majority of Japanese are short of stature, we felt especially tall, which turned out to be an advantage and comfort. In the mass of people thronging the depots I clutched Pammy's hand out of fear that we would become separated. John was easier to spot than Hiro because of his height.

The Japanese stride on hefty sturdy legs, allowing them to disdain railings. Everywhere we climbed endless steps to get to the temple, shrine, or museum. Yet seldom did I see a handrail to secure the descent. At first I felt terribly unsafe, but when I became aware of the thigh muscles I was using, I became enthusiastic. There always remained the chance of breaking your neck though.

The rain at Miyamzhiki, which continued all day long, still was teeming when we went to bed. Hiro said if it cleared, we should be up early to drive to Mt. Fuji. We thought only a miracle could dry up the air enough for a view. When dawn came, the dripping had stopped. Hiro was already dressed and down. We hurried, met the car, and drove to the best vantage point. As we rounded a curve on a hill, Hiro told us to look behind. There stood Mt. Fuji, her snow top glistening in the morning sun, a truly magnificent sight. Though it looks just like the pictures, it seemed far more grandiose and stately. If Hiro had not hustled us off, we would have missed the perfect view. In about a half hour, the clouds rolled in and Mt. Fuji was again hidden from the public. We drove around Lake Hakone, which is a resort, surrounded with hotels, back down through Odawara and other small towns. Again, I was conscious of love of nature in Japan. Even if there is only a foot of ground, you will find a bush, azalea or flower planted.

Everywhere was crowded. Japan was celebrating several national holidays in one week—April 30 was the Emperor's birthday; May Day, May 3 was Constitution Day: and Boy's Day was on May 5. We drove along five miles of beach from which we could see Eno Shima Island. Nearby was the yacht harbor where boat races were held in the Olympics. In the distance, was Oshima Island where 30,000 people live, ignoring the fact that it contains an active volcano. Many commit suicide there each year. At Kamakura, we saw the great Buddha that is forty-two feet tall. A large circle on its forehead signifies illumination of the world.

On Boy's Day, we went to Nikko over night. The train was very crowded. Nikko is as popular in Japan as Niagara Falls is in America. In the morning, it was cold, foggy, and the dampness went deep into our tired bones. Still the shrouds of mist added to the charm, giving it an aura of mystery. At the entrance of the famous shrine was a handsomely carved door (built in 1636) where a priest waved a wand of paper to purify us. Alive with color, it was the most decorative of all the shrines we had seen. Three hundred-year-old cryptomeria trees, resembling our large cedar trees, lined the entrance.

Originally Shintoism and Buddhism were combined. At Nikko, therefore, the Torri Gate is Shinto, and the pagoda is Buddhist. The pagoda has five stories representing five elements. Starting from bottom up, they symbolize earth, water, fire, wind, and heaven. On the Torri Gate were streamers of white paper to purify. Originally these white banners were to keep away flies in Asian countries. It is here you find the famous panel of three monkeys, "See no evil, speak no evil, hear no evil."

Within the buildings, the air was even colder. Even the wool socks didn't help much. For the first time in many, many years, the cemetery of Shoguns was open to the public where the cremated ashes of the important Shoguns were put in coffins. We climbed 240 steps; I counted them, with no railing to help. In the gray eeriness of the fog, the lighting was a proper setting for an ancient cemetery.

We were scheduled to leave Japan at five in the afternoon to fly to Hong Kong. For some reason, we became overly casual at the last. Suddenly, time was short. There was a mad scramble with everyone packing suitcases, finding a taxi for the airport, getting through immigration, and mailing home an overflow of accumulation. I didn't want to take my heavier clothes on to Hong Kong, and there was not enough time to wait in lines at the post office, so I left the matter up to Hiro and the hotel porter. Comparing their estimation with what I had previously shipped home, I knew they were cheating me outrageously, a fact which did not endear me to Hiro. We had already tipped him handsomely. However, there are times when it is useless to discuss a matter. Hiro assured me if there was any money left, he would forward it to me, and I knew this was a farce, he knew it, and he knew I knew it.

Pam was sad about leaving. As we soared away from Tokyo in our Pan American plane, we were fortunate to get a glimpse of Mt. Fuji. It couldn't have been staged better, a fitting goodbye to Japan.

I thought of all we had seen and experienced, the impressions I came away with. On the whole, the Japanese look well fed, happy, and industrious. All cities are churning with activity. On May Day and ordinary days, we had seen demonstrations against the Americans but this seems to happen anywhere in the world.

John had visited a trade show. Contrary to the old belief of Japanese being copiers only, he reported many inventions and ideas originating from this Asian land. They have copied the Western dress but partly, I feel, for practicality. Kimonas, with their elaborate obis, are costly. Certainly wash-and-wear dress is easier to maintain. The Geta (wooden thong sandal) and tabi (one-toed socks) are not as simple as an American shoe. One unique practice is the custom of carrying the baby on their back, a common sight, especially in the rural districts. Babies never cry here. I think it's because they are always with Mama. The people themselves appear prosperous, well fed, and of larger stature than their ancestors. Stores are well-stocked, and streets are crowded. Proof that there are many car owners is the constant snarl of traffic. White-gloved taxi drivers wear chauffeur caps. Disregarding all caution, they wheel recklessly in their anxiety to get you to your destination. Their smiles, giggling faces, and overall politeness seem superficial at times. I feel they have no love for Americans but have tolerated us only, gleaning what they want from us. However, with the exceptions of the demonstrations among students, they gave no concrete evidence of their true feeling. In January 1968, when the Enterprise, a 75,000-ton nuclear-powered U.S. aircraft carrier was scheduled to visit Japan, police had bloody battles with radical Zegakuren students. Other parties, namely the Socialists, the Communists, and Komei Buddhists planned to send out at least 50,000 demonstrators. Let us hope and pray that America and Japan can remain friendly and unite against a deadlier enemy.

The flight to Hong Kong took about four hours. Humid, warm mist greeted our arrival, proof it was getting near the monsoon season. Hong Kong is a British Crown Colony on the southeast coast of China, made up of Hong Kong Island, Peninsula of Kowloon, and the new territories of the mainland and 235 islands. Hong Kong is 29 square miles with a population of 1,200,000. Kowloon is three and a half square miles with a population of over 800,000 people, a great surging mass of humanity.

Again we had a visitor waiting for us when we arrived at the hotel, Henry S., a Chinese gentleman who was acquainted with a friend from home. He also owned a tailor shop. I'm afraid his motives were not all pure. We excused ourselves that night. Early the next morning, Henry called and was waiting below. His demeanor was typically Chinese with an unlimited patience. We breakfasted together. Then, very skillfully, he took us in tow. Sister Helen avoided the whole thing. Morally, we knew we would eventually have to make purchases from Henry. In the meantime, he was very helpful and showed us much. We took the short ride to Kowloon on one of the ferries that leave the docks every few minutes, shuttling back and forth between Hong Kong and Kowloon.

The harbor was fascinating. On view were freighters, a British carrier, and naval ships from every country. Scuttling between the larger vessels were the sampans and the bigger Chinese junks which have a mast and sail. On a typical sampan, you might see a Chinese woman doing all the work. At the same time, with a baby strapped to her back, she may be cooking rice in a corner of the boat.

Chinese are taller and thinner than the Japanese. They rarely smile. Some of the women are beautiful. Many wear the tight, slit skirt associated with the Chinese Mati Hari. Hong Kong is a sprawling city, crowded, and dirty. Millions of people of all kinds and races live there. Most age quickly from hard labor and poor diets.

To further see this city, we took a funicular to the peak that was 1809 feet above sea level. The carrier was similar to an open trolley car, pulled up the perpendicular slope on a cable. There was a police dog that rode first class too, dutifully turning his head to see the spectacular view of Hong Kong, the harbor, and Kowloon peninsula. From this height we would see over to Red China that is twenty-two miles from the ferry dock at Kowloon. At the extreme top of Victoria Mountain is a military radar station, an area closed to the public. A sudden cloud settled like a curtain. We could see nothing. I was glad we had watched the magnificent view while ascending on the tramway. Before the war, the Chinese were not allowed on top of the mountains, only the British. After World War II, anyone who had money could build on the land. There are many large villas sprinkled through the area.

Bamboo is useful as well as ornamental. Asians employ it for scaffolding for new buildings. Tied together with the skin of the bamboo. It looks fragile but, in reality, is very strong. We saw some Catholic churches and monasteries. However, most Chinese are Buddhist. In Hong Kong, they bury the dead in public cemeteries. Graves lay in tiers along the mountainside. After ten years, they dig up the graves, collect the bones, and put them in a jar, feet first. You can see these jars scattered around the hills. Some are resting in the armchair graves that are semi-circular stone monuments. The land known as Hong Kong was formerly China. The 99-year lease to the British would be up in 1998.

I had heard of Aberdeen but thought its description must be exaggerated. You cannot conceive of this life unless you see it for yourself. It is a settlement of at least two thousand people living, eating, and dying on sampans. The boats are in the water, side by side, but never go out to sea. Some people fish, others own shops. No one looked particularly sad or happy. One great mass of humanity is squeezed together, just existing. Even the cats looked hungry and apathetic.

Everywhere you go in settlements, either in squatter's huts or sampans, you see dingy wash hanging out to dry. Probably scarcity of soap and dubious water accounts for the grubby laundry. Many rub clothes on rocks. Hong Kong's water is piped in from Red China. No one suggested it was pure so we drank bottled water while there. The women wear black pants and a tunic that never show the dirt anyway. On their heads they wear a cone-shaped hat of straw. Usually the hair is pinned up or is hanging down the back in one long pigtail. All Chinese have very smooth, hairless skins and fine features. Their hair is thinner than that of the Japanese and not as black.

In May, the warm weather was becoming increasingly humid. For this reason, we tried to do our sightseeing early in the day. We took the ferry over to Kowloon, which means nine dragons. To the Chinese the dragon is a good-luck symbol.

Nathan Road is the main street in Kowloon. Here are assembled hundreds of shops. Probably there are more tailors gathered in one spot here than anywhere else in the world. In the crowded streets, you see the crippled, the blind beggars, and the children peddling their wares. It is not unusual to find men and women sitting on the ground staring blankly. Perhaps they are victims of opium, heroin or other dope. In Asia it is customary to ignore any bodies you might come upon. If you stop to aid a sick or injured man and he dies, you are personally responsible for his burial and doctor bills. Always the Chinese are squatting. They can sit for hours in that position, knees bent, but hips not resting on the ground. There are over one hundred dialects so one district may not understand the next.

After passing Boundary Street, we were in a section called New Territories with Tai Po Road the main street. Here we saw the resettlement buildings that the British built in an effort to eliminate the filth and squalor of the huts. Unfortunately the newer buildings looked no better. There were 2,500 people in each block. Approximately 125,000 men, women, and children resided in this small area. Most of the occupants came from mainland China. Cost of living in these housing units is about fourteen Hong Kong dollars each month. School is not compulsory. Most pay for attending. Consequently many parents put their children to work early, or let them remain idle, wandering in the streets.

Food and materials, such as timber, are all imported. We saw a cargo fleet coming in from Red China, flying the red flag with the five yellow stars. One can still find intricate embroidered cloths and materials in Hong Kong. However, because it is made in China, it is not allowed in the United States. Any embroidery or beaded work must have a certificate of origin to present to customs. Otherwise it is confiscated.

In the countryside, we saw many gardens of lotus roots, vegetables, water chestnuts, and beehives. It was evident that people are more concerned about getting to eat than caring about pretty flowers.

We went to the walled city that is still occupied by older families. All the women were old, toothless, brown, and wrinkled from toiling in the sun. Above the familiar black pants and tunic, they wore Hakka hats made with flat straw brim and open crown. On the edge of the brim hangs a wide ruffle of black material that presumably scares off flies as they move. The water buffalo is used in farming. Pigs, ducks, chicken, and geese are raised for selling.

At the border, we could look over to China. I had imagined a huge wall. A simple barbed-wire fence with a few lookout stations is all that indicates the barrier. The river divides the two areas. Our guide told me he had escaped fifteen years ago by swimming the river at night. He has not dared to go back, though his family is still in China. I like to think the story was true.

At a stopping point, a car backed into our tour car, denting the door. The ensuing argument took up a great deal of time. If no one is hurt in an accident, it is not a police matter. They argued violently while we waited. Because we couldn't understand the language, we didn't know who was winning. I guess both sides knew they had to argue even though the culprit knew he would have to pay the damage. This displayed another example of how difficult it is for the East and West to understand each other.

As we left Hong Kong for Tokyo, Honolulu, and home, I ruminated over all I had seen and heard in the past few weeks. As on any trip, the digesting of it in years to come, affords more pleasure than the actual experience itself. I think the impression, the knowledge that rubs off on your subconscious, the small, funny incidents are all far more important than remembering the historical events in their chronological order.

In thinking of Honolulu, the majority of us visualize beaches, hula dances, and bright sunshine. After Hiroshima, I felt I must also see Pearl Harbor. We took a boat over to Pearl Harbor and the site of the Arizona Memorial, which is a national shrine to the hundreds of men who were trapped inside the battleship Arizona on that fateful December 7, 1941, when the Japanese made their surprise attack on the harbor. As the horrified people on shore watched, the ship sank in nine minutes. Over one thousand men died aboard. About two hundred escaped. Five battleships were lost that day and many damaged.

At the Arizona Memorial the flag is raised and lowered each day. Hundreds of visitors come. Although I had no personal connection with the Arizona or Pearl Harbor, it is a sobering experience and one I shall never forget, standing in silent salute to those Americans who died there. I could understand the cry, "Remember Pearl Harbor." My eyes filled with unexpected tears. Pam grasped my hand and said, "I know now what you meant in Hiroshima."

In Honolulu, a degree of relaxation was accomplished. Three days later, laden with traditional leis, we waved goodbye to dear friends. The flight home seemed shorter. Each of us was quiet, deep in personal thought and remembrance of the past weeks.

6

ANIMALS

Our career with animals has been varied and not wholly successful. As a child, I was terrified of dogs. We always had huge ones too. My earliest encounter was with the family collie, a gigantic furry creature that could knock me down easily and often did. Dad offered me a reward if one day I would take the collie for a walk, on a leash, the entire length of the street. Because it was a very long street, this was a difficult decision. It took several weeks to rouse enough courage to make the attempt. To be truthful, it was not one hundred percent successful either.

On the return trip, just yards from home, we met another massive dog, and I was incapable of hanging on to the leash. I ran sobbing to the front door, Dad was very understanding, did not score against me for the ignominious ending. Although this venture did not allay my fears, I felt that I had conquered partly a former insurmountable obstacle.

Airedales were much in vogue when I was small. We had a series of them. Most were dumb, destructive, and chewers. I could not admire them. Even the names were unimaginative. Now, I cannot distinguish one dog from another. Only one, Rags, do I remember. He was distinctive because he loved to eat sweaters and pounce on them and clomp off delightedly for a good wooly chew.

I well remember Happy, a large combination collie and sheepdog with whom I felt more comfortable. He was strictly the outdoor type. To my way of thinking that is where a dog should be.

At this time, the family lived in the country in summer, and in the city in winter, resulting in confusion for all. One September night we were exhausted from the moving to town. Suddenly we realized Happy was not thumping his tail on the porch. Everyone yodeled, looking fearfully down the street. Perhaps he had been stricken ill or hit by an automobile.

On a hunch, Dad rode out to the country and there was Happy, foot sore and tired, sitting patiently by the front gate. Happy's affectionate, warm personality made him beloved by young and old. When he died of old age, he was mourned by family and neighbors alike.

I guess I am not what you'd call a genuine animal lover. We had a brief encounter with the horse routine. One summer when sister and I were sixteen and thirteen respectively, the family rented a sophisticated horse named "Blackie." Sister Barby wasn't wildly enthusiastic either. Since she was older and busier, it was up to me to keep Blackie in shape. I hated the sweat he lathered up, and the manure. Blackie was always my master. Periodically, he tossed me off, and I had to walk home.

In later years, when we had our own children, a friend's pony, Dan, boarded with us for the summer. Dan was another ornery independent animal. Short and fat, he bucked and kicked, I sincerely believe just for the hell of it. One day, when he was being particularly obstinate, the children and neighbor children came to me anxiously. "We want to ride Dan," they said, "but he won't let us."

I wished secretly the whole moment could disappear, taking Dan with it. However, I realized this was a supreme test, a chance to prove my authority and superiority over beast. How I hated that pony for putting me in this ridiculous predicament. Praying silently, I mounted Dan, and we charged back and forth on the front lawn like the "White Tornado" of the television ad. The children were properly impressed. With a word to be "firm," I returned triumphantly to the safety of my own kitchen. Needless to say, I never repeated the performance. The memory of my success served me well.

Cocker spaniels were popular for a while. John and I owned a red thorough-bred named Corky, whom we had bought from the furrier. Corky was a lot of trouble, highly bred, and jittery. Each night his silky red hair was filled with burrs and thorns. Daily grooming was an absolute must. That job fell to me. A fussy eater, he preferred, demanded, and received only the higher priced cuts of beef.

Trusting this dog to be completely housebroken, I was appalled one day, while visiting my mother-in-law, to see Corky wander up to the grandfather clock, lift his hind leg and relieve himself.

Later, despite the shots, he came down with distemper. Days of hospitaliza-tion followed. When the veterinarian called me and said, "You might as well take him home to die. He's unhappy here." At home, no one ever received more solic-itous care. With a spoon I fed him such delicacies as fresh squeezed beef juice and coddled eggs. With hourly feeding, love, and rest, he recovered.

At this time, we bought a black female with the intention of raising spaniels as a sideline. One dark, rainy night, Corky got run over by a truck. No cocker spaniel could take Corky's place. In our grief, we gave away the female and decided to change breed if we bought any more dogs.

Again we were living in the country in a charming but very old house that we tried to modernize. One major objection we could not overcome was the age of the house with its old walls. Efforts of the exterminator could not rid us of the river rats who could get in between the walls.

Following a particularly restless night, we consulted the farmer who did some plowing for us. "I'll lend you our cat." He said. "Best ratter in the whole country side." He advised us to lock up the cat in the basement without food. "Your rats will be gone in two days." He solemnly vowed.

At the end of one day, I thought it strange there were no meowings or scratch-ings. On investigation, there was no sign of the monstrous yellow tomcat we had confined. A few tufts of fur were the only evidence of his existence. Shocked, we searched every corner of the cellar. Next we visited all the neighbors. Nobody had seen the Davis cat.

Unbelievable as it was, we finally came to the conclusion that the rats had eaten the cat! The hardest part of this was telling the farmer and his children. Although we paid him money, it in no way compensated for the loss of their pet. It was a harrowing experience, my first with a cat. I harbored no real fondness for felines, but such a fate horrified me.

Topper was an adorable, completely undependable dog with a huge black cir-cle surrounding one eye that gave him a jaunty look. A complete screwball, he was friendly to all, loyal to no one. He often wandered off, adopting new families, miles away. When we raced over to pick him up, we felt morally obligated to reward the people who had befriended the dog. Topper was delighted with the publicity and attention but made no attempt to reform. Eventually we were forced to give him away, as the performance proved too costly and nerve-wrack-ing.

Later there was Duke, a black and white English Setter. Such a handsome creature he was that even I was impressed. John was ecstatic. Simultaneously, we acquired a new station wagon. My husband had great visions of driving around in it with Duke sitting aristocratically in the rear. On the first try, Duke started drooling and looking at us with desperate brown eyes. We stopped the car and let him out to recover. Unfortunately, this was not a thing to which he became accustomed. Duke always got carsick. After several trials, we had to abandon the fine image of station wagon with setter.

One afternoon, when I was home alone, I heard tires screeching and a loud thud. Instinctively, I knew our dog had been hit. Running out, I saw nothing.

After a brief search, I found him, under a bush, conscious but breathing heavily. I phoned the doctor for help. He said he could do nothing about transporting him. However, he wanted me to get him there as fast as I could, adding that more dogs died of shock than the actual injury.

I was home alone. Speed was the primary factor. Somehow, with that hidden strength we all have, I heaved him in the station wagon. I'm sure I hurt him, but he realized I was trying to help. He didn't cry.

The next week was hideous. Duke rallied, then sank. Each day we dreaded making the call. As each night passed though, we came to realize his chances of survival were better. Many weeks and many dollars later, we were able to bring him home. Lame from the accident, he still retained his sweet disposition.

When Pam was born, Duke suddenly assumed the responsibility of her guardianship. First he nipped the milkman. Then ensued the week of observation at the doctor's, waiting the possibility of rabies. Next, he tore the pants of the department store delivery man. More doctor bills. I stopped all deliveries.

When he attacked the diaper man, I did the laundry myself. Repeated incidents eventually led to the momentous decision. Either the baby left or we disposed of the dog!

One offer for our pet was on a street with traffic. Another potential owner had a disagreeable manner. After rejecting several suggestions, the vet came up with one that seemed fitting. He wanted to keep Duke at the kennels, using him as a blood donor when accidents occurred. My close relationship with the dog had a deep effect on me. I never saw him again. I couldn't bear to see him penned up for life.

Our dear friend Charlie, had a female cat, Mittens, who produced great litters of kittens regularly. Cats were an enigma to me. I had never owned one, nor did I want to. However, in a weak moment, I accepted one of the kittens. Having observed the prolific habits of Mittens, with the accompanying difficulty of disposing of the offspring, I insisted on a male. I questioned Charlie closely on this matter. "Best boy of the lot," he assured me.

In an unbelievably short time, I discovered our "male kitten" was pregnant. Unabashed, Charlie admitted it was sometimes difficult to determine the sex when they were very young. Resigned to our fate, I rationalized by telling myself it would be educational for the children. I was ignorant on ways of cats. One day Tuppence, our pregnant kitty, was missing.

I called, frantically. What if she had her litter out in the field? I ran around excitedly, looking under beds. Suddenly, I heard some tissue rustling. In a box, on top of my new hat, lay Tuppence, giving birth to wet, squirming kittens. Not a child in sight to witness this miracle of birth. Box and blanket so carefully prepared for the event, remained empty. By the time the children returned, the new mother had cleaned up her babies. It seemed reasonably safe to move them to their box. The new hat went into the incinerator!

Tuppence was a disagreeable cat with a strange personality. Climbing up my best drapes, she pulled threads with her claws. She was an impossible mother, extremely cold and rough with the newborn.

In a month's time, the kittens had grown enormously. "What to do with them?" Everyone I approached suddenly developed an allergy to cats. The excuses varied, but the fact remained that no one wanted a new kitten. We decided to keep one, a haughty yellow giant tomcat, whom we named Charles II. Homes were finally found for the rest. What a relief!

Nature being what it is, a few months later, we had the same problem all over again. Each time Tuppence gave birth, she was more than generous about it, producing five, six, and even seven at a time. Because of the cat's personality quirk, she was not popular with family or friends.

Once, we went to Put-In-Bay to visit my sister-in-law. Karen, the rightful owner of this feline creature, refused to leave her behind. So we rented a cat carrier and took Tuppence with us. "But my dog just hates cats." She wailed. "He trees them every time." Tuppence remained in a closet most of the weekend. I know the cat would have been happier at the vet's. She was terrified of the ferry ride, hated the confinement of the carrier. We were all relieved to return home with the animal still alive.

In time, we found a recipient for Tuppence and her newest family on a farm where cats were welcome to rid the barns of rodents. This left us with Charles II who was a pleasant, healthy animal. He and Duke, the English setter, were best of friends, partaking of the same supper. At night, Duke allowed Charles to nestle between his front paws. Charles also became a soft pillow for the dog.

Mother cared for the children and Charles while we went on a football weekend. Belatedly, I realize what an imposition that was. Children she adored but not a great tomcat. When I returned, Charles was sans voice. A violent fight must have taken place, leaving the cat torn, silent but with spirit intact. I became fond of Charles who was affectionate without becoming a pest.

Another weekend, we left with children. Charles was in custody of the girl next door. We never saw him again. Now I believe he was killed by older jealous tomcats. His image haunted me. Each time I saw a yellow cat, I doubled back for a second look. In time we learned to accept the obvious truth. Charles had departed to a better world.

French poodle entered our life. We bought a six-week-old female. From acquaintances, I heard the dos and don'ts of poodle care. This lovable puppy, Muffy, was happy, friendly, but impossible to train. Literally, I spent hours taking her out on a leash night and day. Sometimes she would cooperate but I despaired of ever housebreaking her.

When she was six months old, she was killed by a hit and run driver. Unfortunately, she didn't die immediately. I heard the impact. Wrapping her in a blanket, I raced to the vet's. They tried. However, she was badly hurt internally, and died two days later.

Scooter is a silky black cat with a touch of white at the throat. He has been with us for over eleven years. Without a doubt he has managed to be the most costly animal of all. A plain ordinary cat with no fancy pedigrees, he lived a kingly existence. When we go away, he boards in deluxe, air-conditioned quarters at the kennels. Scooter is independent. On occasion, he condescends to a brief caress or stroking. Whenever I am on the verge of becoming fond of him, he will leap at me, tearing my stocking. If I don't feed him when his stomach tells him it's time, he sometimes nips me on the leg with his needle-like teeth.

I could not describe him as a cuddly cat. Nevertheless, if I let him roam at night, he will scratch the door to be let in the bedroom. A houseguest was badly frightened when this furry brat jumped on her bed in the middle of the night. For this reason we put him in the basement at bedtime where he has a three-room suite, including the well-furnished recreation room. In a Houdini-like performance with his paw on one side while holding the other door secure. It takes a series of barricades to keep him in at night.

Last fall, for several mornings he didn't appear when I loosened the locks to let him out. He looked old and sick with sagging stomach. Alarmed, I took him to the vet. Five days and forty-five dollars later, he was released with the diagnosis "arthritis". He's been fine ever since. I suspect Scooter put on the whole act just for attention or spite.

Another time he arrived at the door, limping badly, holding his right front paw at an awkward angle. A trip to the vet's confirmed my suspicion of a leg fracture. Solitary confinement was the order. Even with this precaution, he developed a leg ulcer and had an extended stay at the cat hospital. The bill for this ailment was one hundred dollars and forty-five cents. Our cold-blooded yardman said, "Why don't you just put him to sleep?" I didn't speak to him for several hours.

Karen had a fondness for goldfish which invariably died. I never knew how noisy goldfish are until I slept in her room one night. They suck, smack, and swish around in their glass cage all night long.

One morning, Karen found two dead goldfish. She planned an elaborate funeral with solemn burial. Returning from school, she found that Mary, the cleaning lady, had flushed them down the toilet in her absence. Karen never forgave any of us for allowing that incident to happen.

Turtles had a place in our home for a while too. Their lifespan was longer than goldfish, but it was just as disconcerting to find one swimming in the bathtub or basin. One of the most popular turtles was Terry who belonged to our youngest. His demise was a difficult for her to accept. He had a beautiful funeral service. Burial in a velvet lined box was under the big oak by the lake in Michigan.

At the onset of life with Scooter, our blackest cat, we sought the advice of the vet. I related to him the sad ending of Charles II. I learned that undoubtedly Charles had been killed by the older male cats that resented and feared the popularity of a handsome young tomcat. "If you want to have a pet, it is wisest to have the male altered or de-sexed." Therefore, Scooter's sex life is not an active one. Perhaps this is why he gets so ornery at times. All in all, he's an interesting pet. Haughty, independent, nonetheless, he remains loyal to the family.

One summer in Michigan when Scooter was about six years old, we lost him for a frightening four days. Pammy walked down the road, peering in the woods and, between sobs, called his name repeatedly. We alerted neighbors, advertised in the papers, even announced his loss on the radio. Imagining I heard his meow, I arose innumerable times in the night to let him in. No black cat was visible.

During the fifth night of his absence, a violent thunderstorm raged. No one could sleep. Shortly after midnight, I thought I heard a cat crying. Half-heartedly I went to the door. There stood Scooter, shivering and thin but alive. No cat has ever had a more cordial welcome. After that experience, we were careful to get him in before dark. To this day, his absence is a mystery. Either he was treed by a wild animal, lost his way, or tangled with a skunk. All of these are conjectures of course. Only Scooter knows the truth.

Our last experience with a dog had discouraged me permanently I think. "Poodles" was an apricot-colored French poodle belonging to a friend, Mrs. W. A new baby in their household was usurping Poodle's place, with tragic results. The dog reverted to infantile habits himself, ignoring the fact that he had been housebroken. Extremely jealous of the baby, his behavior became insufferable. Mrs. W. asked me if I knew anyone dopey enough to take him. "Me", I answered weakly. This was shortly after Muffy's demise. I was feeling softly sentimental.

"He also likes to sleep in someone's bedroom," my friend cautioned. Sharing a bedroom with animals never had appealed to me. However, within a week, Poodles had left the cold, slated floor of the front hall, and was now luxuriating comfortably on my best bathrobe next to my bed.

My husband hooted at the name of Poodles. We switched to Poudeau, which retained the French flavor without confusing the dog too much. Poudeau was a lovable patient friend for eight years in our house. His manners did not reach perfection. As long as we stayed at home, he behaved. When we went out, he had an accident (on purpose). Sternly I scolded and pleaded. Poudeau remained boss. Firmly implanted in his mind was one thought. "If they ignore me, they deserve punishment. They quickest way to get attention is to ruin their best carpet."

Poudeau was gentle and kind. His car manners were poor though. I see many dogs waiting quietly in the car while the owner does errands. One poodle I knew waits through eighteen holes of golf. Not Poudeau! The first time I took him with me, I stopped for a quick errand at the store. Poudeau barked continuously, slobbering on the windows, and clawing at the upholstery. He never learned. Once we stopped at a sandwich shop. Poudeau created such a fuss; I finally bought him a hamburger and took it to him in the car. Even this did not suffice. He thought it showed discrimination by not being at the table with us.

During the first summer Poudeau accompanied us to the lake in Michigan. We discovered he couldn't swim. We fastened a child's life preserver on his back when in the boat, which made people point and laugh. Eventually Pam taught him to swim. But, though poodles claim to be originally water dogs, Poudeau displayed a distinct aversion to water in any form. Even when thirsty, he avoided the lake, preferring to wait until someone filled his water dish.

Our apricot poodle had a delightful way of begging for food. It was tough refusing to capitulate to his pleas. Sitting straight up on his hind legs, cocking his head to one side, he silently stared with his huge shiny, brown eyes. For endless stretches, he sat this way, front paws together as if in prayer. What made it doubly appealing was the silence. By eliminating the barking, he commanded more sympathy than ever. Whenever we had a party, he was delighted. This soulful stance was certain to arouse the compassion of at least one guest. No matter how I warned, inevitably there would be one softhearted person who later said, "I couldn't resist giving him a snack—he begged so politely." Yes, he was a clever dog.

Although I was irritated constantly by Poudeau's eccentricities and shortcomings, I loved him. His gruesome end was death by a German Shepard dog. Poudeau was badly mangled. Unfortunately he lived for several hours. A death of old age, we could have accepted in time. This bloody, undignified passing left us horrified. Even Scooter was affected. In fact, I believe that his own traumatic experience of the broken leg was somehow related to the same vicious dog.

It was many months before the cat mustered courage to venture outside again. Creeping as far as the door, he cautiously poked out his head, peering right and left. At the slightest noise, he backed hurriedly into the house. As Pam suggested, "Too bad they don't have psychiatrists for cats."

Presently our animals are reduced to two, Scooter and Judy. Judy is a magnificent horse, sensitive, spirited but at the same time, gentle. I do not understand horses one bit. I keep my distance.

I recall staying at a dude ranch in Arizona years ago. To be invited to clean the corral was a degree of status for which all guests strive—all but me. I couldn't believe it was true. Women were thrilled to have the opportunity to shovel manure and spread hay!

Judy belongs to my husband. To him, she is part of the family. He rides all year, regardless of weather. Fox hunting from August to December is important. Pammy does not hunt but rides beautifully. With her sensitive touch, she handles strong horses better than many men. Judy is close to her too. And the last of our animals.

7

FRIENDS

How many friends do you have? What is a real friend? Many of us have asked these questions. During a lifetime, everyone comes in contact with a great many people. Unless you are in solitary confinement, undoubtedly you have a quantity of acquaintances. The need for more is in most of us—a friend, a confidante, another human being we can trust.

A lonely child will wail, "I want someone for a best friend." A frustrated woman will moan, "I need someone to talk with." We all want the warm feeling of being needed. A close friend is a rare treasure to be highly valued. It is even more unusual to have <u>one</u> best friend all your life. Circumstances and events change us all. You may have a pal you enjoy sports with. You may have a companion with whom you share religious experiences. You may have a friend whose husband is compatible with yours. Regardless of your status, I venture to say the number of really true, close friends remains a small one.

My first best friend was found in kindergarten. Dad did not enter me in the fall. He had a far-out idea that he would undertake my education. By February, Mother was sick of the whole experiment and enrolled me in a girl's school. Naturally shy, it was terrifying to enter the classroom where everyone was already acquainted. One freckle-faced, red-haired girl, Frances Henshaw, marched up to me. Solemnly taking my hand, she coaxed me over to a chair by her. For the next five years, we were best friends.

In summer, the Henshaws moved to the country. Looking back, I can well understand Mrs. Henshaw's reluctance to approach June and the summer months. The help was not happy away from the city, so everything was on a tight schedule. Meals were served promptly. If we didn't get up in time, we cooked our own breakfast and washed the dishes.

For me, the Henshaw farm was a joy to visit. At the side of the house was a pond with an old rowboat and canoe for our pleasure. Frances and her younger brother also were the proud owners of a pony and cart. We were allowed to ride to the village for ice cream cones. Because of the vertical hill up to Henshaws, the return trip was not as carefree. Usually we had to get out of the cart half way up the incline, leading and coaxing the pony the rest of the way. He was a small Shetland, well behaved, but the long steep terrain was a strain on all of us.

Included in the wealth of child entertainment, was a small swimming pool, a novelty and luxury in those days, especially in the country. Spring-fed, it required several days to fill it with the icy water. Little was known of the care of swimming pools in those days. Circulation or self-cleaning devices were unheard of which resulted in many problems. By the middle of the summer, the pool was slimy, dark green. Frogs, tadpoles, and occasionally a snake had to be fished out. None of this bothered any of us. Scientifically, it was not most hygienic, but no one suffered.

The older girls had their boy friends for swimming parties while we stood around and watched wistfully. The pool was at the bottom of a hill also, a long climb back to the house. During heavy rains, the surface water rushed down to add to the already polluted pool.

Incongruously, with all these luxuries, Frances preferred to come to our house. This seemed ridiculous to me, as there was nothing to do there but roller skate or play jacks. Somehow Frances and I drifted apart. She remained solemn, cryptic, and antisocial. At seventh grade, she went away to school. Our close relationship was dissolved.

For a brief period, Mary Frick was my best friend. Her older brother had a crush on me, so it was fun to visit her. The Fricks had a swimming pool also, in town, and it was the gathering place for all the young people. Mrs. Frick was austere, sharp, and strict. Her four children paid her little attention. Though she kept trying valiantly, her control was nil. According to rumor, Mr. Frick had a mistress in another city. Seldom was he home.

Mary was not a true friend. I was naïve, flattered by her attention. When we were alone with girls, she monopolized my time. If a boy appeared on the scene, she behaved like a female bird, strutting and preening. In a bathing suit, her figure was superb. At the pool she had all the boys after her.

Once I gave a supper party for boys and girls that turned out to be a melee. Literally chasing the boys, playing catch with the olives and pickles, she did anything for attention. It was contagious. Excitement mounted as Mary, spurred on by her success, proceeded to ensnare one boy after another. Many of the girls were abandoned by their dates. Helplessly they watched, as Mary remained the belle of the party throughout dinner and dancing later.

When Mary went away to boarding school, I turned to Eleanor who was my best friend through high school. We shared confidences until I learned she was repeating my secrets. This was the final shattering of my faith in the female species. We remained good friends, but I learned to keep quiet. Many confided in me because they learned of my ability to keep a secret. "I can tell you, Edna, because I know you won't repeat it," became a familiar phrase to my ears. It was a strain. I received many confessions I did not want to be burdened with. Through the years it was the same confessions of abortion, sordid love affairs, secret bouts of drinking. I hope the telling of it lessened the pain for some of those tortured. It made me feel like a priest though I knew little advice to offer. I did not become a recluse or bitter, but I did become cautious. Perhaps many of us keep a part of us locked away. To some extent we are all superficial.

The one girl who remained a friend was my cousin, Joan. We were brought up together, though we didn't live in the same house. I was expected to be the leader, take care of her. From the beginning, we were separate identities, not copying each other, not always agreeing, but ever a deep mutual understanding, the rare beauty of a true friendship.

When I was about ten, we had a club that was exclusive, just Joan and I. Ten-cent dues were required at our Thursday meeting. Once, meeting day came on the same day as my class birthday party. It never occurred to us to postpone the club, and we just excused ourselves and held our meeting. We wrote stories and articles with the thought that someday we would publish. To Joan the weekly assignment was a burden. Possessor of a marvelously active imagination, her youth prevented her from expressing it all easily, let alone write it legibly.

Joan was the middle child. Sometimes she felt abandoned. Her oldest brother was the delight of her mother. Baby sister needed attention. Joan turned to me for comfort, advice, and help. When she was recuperating from chicken pox, brother Don contracted pneumonia, so Joan stayed at our house. I washed her hair and treated the remaining pox scabs. She was sent to overnight camp where I had already spent a year. There I looked after her, remembering my own homesickness the previous summer.

Once Joan packed her suitcase and came to our house. "I'm running away," she announced.

"Why?" I asked, startled.

"No one loves me at home." She answered simply. I was appalled. Such a move not only would not occur to me, but I would have lacked the daring to carry it out. Furthermore, I was safe, protected, and content at home. I didn't want to run away. I pointed out to Joan that it was foolish to stay at our house because Mother would just call her mother anyway. "Well, I'll run away to Cousin Bella's then," Joan said. She phoned Bella who lived in a little country home about twenty miles away. Bella persuaded her to postpone her visit until she was older.

For a long while, I was in awe of Joan for her braveness in getting as far as packing the suitcase. Most of my friends made wild threats of assaults or retribution on their parents that they knew and I knew would not be carried out. Somehow just voicing the injustice or frustration made it fade in importance.

I was at Joan's overnight when she had her first menstrual period. She shrieked with horror. I went running. Her mother had prepared her no better than mine. It took all evening to convince her she was all right, normal and not bleeding to death.

Many times I could not give her the answers she sought. At camp, she developed an eczema condition on the inside of her arm. At that point, she was attempting the study of Christian Science, relying on her faith to clear it up. When the eruption did not vanish immediately, she came to me with many complex questions of God, the Universe, and mind over matter. I felt lost and inadequate.

Religion to me had been Sunday School and stereotyped church services. It was disturbing to realize suddenly that there were many unanswered questions in my mind also. We floundered through the subject together. If nothing else, at least I could listen. Joan was inquisitive and searching, which stimulated my own thinking. We came to no startling conclusions, but both of us benefited from the discussions.

Joan started dating at an early age, as I did, so our lives continued together although we were of different ages groups and schools. When she didn't find what she was seeking in a friend, she returned to me.

Joan attended college briefly. Then she worked for a while in a department store. Long hours of standing played havoc with her health. She developed painful hemorrhoids and backaches and became thin and nervous. Of course, simultaneously, she was going out in the evening which added to her weariness.

At college, the roommate I abhorred on sight, turned out to be my best friend for those years. From Nebraska, Molly's entrance in the eastern college was her first experience away from her home territory. She hated it. Molly was a tall redhead with green eyes and freckles.

In contrast to my former ways, I wasted much time at college trying to take the easy courses. I discovered later that if the subject doesn't interest you, it could well turn out to be the most difficult one. Molly had learned all this. Plunging directly into the curriculum, she signed up for German, Psychology, and Math. Her grades were high, and she enjoyed the courses. Cursing at my stupidity, I struggled with philosophy, which I hated. Government consisted of attending boring lectures with emphasis on outside reading.

Molly's background and interests were different from mine. However, we soon reached a common plane and became fast friends. I secured dates for her. If I was late getting in at night, she covered up for me.

Molly needed a lot of sleep and had the knack of relaxing quickly. After an early class, she raced back to the room. Stretching out on the cot, she would say, "Wake me for my eleven o'clock class." Within seconds she was sound asleep. I marveled at this art. Perhaps the reason she needed the rest was that she was prone to sleep walking. At midnight she might jump to her feet, start to brush her hair vigorously or wriggle into her clothes. Once, she ran to the phone booth with me after her to keep her from falling down stairs. She never remembered these night wanderings. My rest was constantly interrupted, but I didn't mind.

After two years, Molly transferred to UCLA. Desperately I wanted to go too. This suggestion produced a flood of mail from home, all containing reasons of disapproval. Even Grandmother wrote and begged me to stay in the East. "You might marry a Californian and break your father's heart." In these days, we more or less followed the dictates of our elders.

I didn't see Molly again for fourteen years. Our correspondence had dwindled to nothing, each of us caught in our own snarled lives. In fact, I wasn't sure where she lived. During World War II my husband and I took a trip to the West Coast. Per usual, I studied the phonebook at each stop. I discovered Molly was living right in Hollywood! Excitedly we made a date to meet.

I know each of us spent hours primping, dreading to admit the change that marriage, children, and housework had wrought. Miraculously, we were able to take up right where we left off. Years slipped together in one brief moment. This friendship was rekindled several times, but the last attempt was a failure.

Molly had divorced her husband and had been going steady with a man who had no intention of marrying her. Her daughter had made an unfortunate marriage and was now living in Mexico. We had both changed too much over the years. Inevitably the former rapport between us was gone. I shed a few tears over it but vowed to dismiss the past. Often we cannot change the ravages of time or life itself, and cannot recapture the once precious moments.

Did you ever try to maintain a friendship with one of the opposite sex? If you are over six years of age, it is not successful. Much as we like to think we can do as we please, be independent, for we are all creatures of convention. People do not believe a woman's friendship with a man. No matter how beautiful or comforting such a relationship is, someone will sully it with talk of an affair, a romance, or a sex angle. This usually hurts not only the two involved, but their friends or family too.

My cousin Joan and I continued living in the same city after our respective marriages. We didn't go as a foursome, but the life-long attachment between the two of us continued. She phoned me several times a day: "How do you clean liver?" "What shall I do for Jenny's rash?" Sometimes she just wanted to chat nonsense or reminisce. If I was busy, she rang off instantly. But she called back later.

Joan complained of a scratchy throat during the summer of 1966. Unfortunately, the doctor took the matter lightly. Joan often suffered from minor ailments which, in fact, could be attributed to over indulgence in smoking or drinking. This in no way exonerated the doctor, of course. Part of the trouble today is the lack of interest or compassion in another human being.

By October, Joan was in the hospital undergoing extensive treatment for cancer of the throat. Simultaneously, I was in a hospital out of town, recovering from a fractured neck caused by a freak accident.

When I returned by hospital plane and ambulance and was sufficiently strong to walk with a cane, I wanted to see her. Instinctively, I knew the surgery she was facing would mean a drastic laryngectomy. With my husband protesting all the while, we maneuvered the journey to her hospital bed where we had a brief visit together.

The radical surgery left her voiceless. For one who was naturally garrulous, it was a double frustrating trauma. Determined to overcome this handicap, she took lessons from the speech and hearing center. However, she never spoke again.

After a brief respite, cancer struck again. This time it attacked her lung. Despite heavy cobalt treatment, the disease was not conquered. Neither doctor nor family told her the truth. When my father was dying of cancer, I asked the attending physician about telling the patient his condition. He told me, "Eddie, it's a game we all play. Family doesn't want the suffering loved one to know. In the end, the victim always knows but wants to spare the family."

Watching a loved one die by inches is devastating. You feel so helpless. I visited her regularly, sometimes every day. Many criticized me for such constant attention. I consulted a life-long friend, a minister. "Keep it up," he counseled. "Too often people get careless, leave a friend to die alone." Reassured, I doubled my efforts to think of ways to brighten a moment, a gift to make her more comfortable.

Joan's husband gave up his job to devote himself entirely to her comfort and welfare, attending to her night and day. One day he fell sick himself. Even without my scolding, I think they realized they would need nurses. Dick engaged two, but continued to care for her personally half the time, rarely leaving the house.

Her husband tried everything to make her life easier. A stairway elevator was installed which she never used. He supervised her food, coffee, and ice cream for breakfast, mashed avocado for lunch. Anything fattening that could be swallowed with ease was made available.

Three months before she died, she asked me to come over one particular day. She gave me a tiny antique vase filled with a sprig of ivy and a fresh bachelor button. "This is one of my most treasured possessions." She said. "I want you to have it. I love you very much. You have always taken care of me and been around when I need you."

These words I shall always remember. As so often is the case, I am convinced she knew she was going to die and when.

The daughter living at home waited on her mother with a gentle touch. Joan developed painful bedsores despite all precautions. Her body was a mere skeleton, covered with a thin layer of skin. I doubt that she weighed more than fifty pounds. I don't know why or how she was allowed to live in this condition. I feel she tried to hang on desperately for the sake of her husband.

A few days before Christmas in 1968, she mercifully slid into a coma. I stopped on a Saturday afternoon, but she was impervious to sound or voice. A few minutes later, she slipped into another more peaceful life, without a struggle. Simply her breathing stopped. Her daughter cried, and we clung to each other. I think both her husband and I had done most of our mourning during the past two years. You cannot wish for such a hopeless existence to continue.

Now, I experience a great loss and inquietude in many ways. My last close link with childhood is gone. My one life-long friend is gone. Presently the feeling of being needed is removed. I mourn for the unfinished life she led, the missions unaccomplished, the time wasted, the deeds undone.

One thing stands out above all else. The love and devotion between husband and wife in this case is a rare commodity. Many men will unhesitatingly provide the best for their mate. How many will take on the actual physical and emotional wants of their loved one on a twenty-four hour basis? Joan used to complain of Dick's watchdog attitude. "I remonstrated mildly, reminding her of how good he was to her. She said simply, "I would do the same for him and have."

As the song goes, "People need people." Good close friends are few. The older we get, the more changes occur. But we cannot go it alone. We need God and another human being to make our life meaningful.

978-0-595-37073-3
0-595-37073-X

www.ingramcontent.com/pod-product-compliance
Lightning Source LLC
Chambersburg PA
CBHW051449280526
45785CB00003B/1484